THE JOB HUNTING BOOK

Career mentoring and job seeking tips
– graduate edition

IAN ALLAN

For intern, new graduate and early career
job seekers. Includes worked examples of
résumés for an...

- Entry level job in Marketing
- Entry level job in IT
- Entry level job in Accounting

National Library of Australia Cataloguing-in-Publication data: Creator:	Allan. Ian. 1963 – author.
Title:	The Job Hunting Book Ian Allan.
Subtitle:	Career mentoring and job seeking tips – graduate edition
ISBN:	EPUB: 978-0-6454465-3-1 Paperback: 978-0-6454465-4-8 Hardback: 978-0-6454465-5-5
Notes:	Includes table of contents.
Subjects:	Resume Job hunting Self help Career

Book design and layout by Sandy Coventry, Nitty Gritty Graphics, nittygrittygraphics.com.au
Cover designby Vanessa Mendozzi

Disclaimer
The material in this publication is general in nature only. It does not represent professional advice. Everybody's circumstances are different. If expert assistance is required, the service of an appropriate professional should be sought. To the maximum extent permitted by law, the author and publisher disclaim all responsibility and liability to any person, arising directly or indirectly from them taking or not taking action based on the information in this publication.

Ian Allan is not affiliated with and does not endorse any of the corporate entities mentioned in or involved in the distribution of this work, or any third party entities whose trademarks and logos may appear on this work.

Quantity sales
Special discounts are available on quantity purchases by corporations, associations, and others. Special print runs that include with compliments from [your business] can also be arranged. For details, contact me at ian@ianallanauthor.com

Contents

Contents continued

List of figures

List of tables

About the Author – Ian Allan

Life has a way of throwing up challenges. Mine happened in my late teens. In the final year of my apprenticeship a nasty workplace accident forced me to rethink my career.

Fast forward to my early 30s, I'd been a furniture restorer, a furniture removalist, a bingo caller, a pedestrian accident researcher, a condom tycoon (for some reason that failed to impress my girlfriend's mother), a software engineer, and a lecturer and researcher in mapping science. I won jobs, sometimes due to my tenacity, but looking back, mostly through word of mouth.

In the 90s I started a consultancy and did map modelling for universities, the water industry, all levels of the Australian government and the UN. Magically, consulting work and now my employees came via word of mouth.

So, after 40 years as an employee and as a consultant, I've learnt that the secret sauce for getting work is relationships, especially professional relationships. These need not be insincere or manipulative. Opportunities naturally arise if you make the effort. The trick to giving relationships their best chance of yielding work is to put yourself in the other person's boots and empathize with their problems, their hopes and their dreams. Getting work becomes a simpler exercise when you've customized your offering to meet someone's needs. And that, in a nutshell, is what this book is about.

I'm a teacher at heart. Now, in my 50's, I can look back on my career as an employee looking for work, as a consultant winning work, and as an employer hiring and firing. When I started out, the guidance I give you in the following pages was not around for me. In the absence of a mentor, I had to work it out for myself. And so here it is for you. For all you early career job seekers, I hope *The Job Hunting Book* makes your job seeking journey an easier one.

Preface

PARALLEL UNIVERSE #1
– ALEX HASN'T READ THIS BOOK YET.

Job hunting is frustrating. This must be Alex' one hundredth job application. Alex has downloaded a résumé template from the web, filled it in, and by changing the job and employers details, has been very efficient and emailed it to five employers just today.

Lou is overworked and understaffed. The right employee would take the pressure off. The responses from last week's ad keep coming in. Over two hundred already. Evaluating them is another job on top of everything else. It wouldn't be so bad if they were all killer candidates, but so far, they all seem hell-bent on sabotaging their chances. None have made the effort to address Lou's carefully crafted job description, so only a few have made it into the *maybe* pile.

Returning from a break, Lou sits down to check more emails. *Spam, spam, spam, spam. Oh. Here's one. My new employee perhaps? Bla, bla, bla...promising...résumé attached...hmmm...*

I bet they emailed this to 20 employers just today...Lets give them the benefit of doubt...Check them out on LinkedIn. Ahhhhh! Just as I thought. Alex is a "student at a university". Nothing more. Why bother? There's time I'll never get back!

Even good people have bad days, and it's one of those days for Lou.

People talking about job seeking are like teenagers talking about sex. Most proclaim to be experts. Some have success stories to tell. Others, failure stories. Others are conspicuously quiet. There's lots of talk. Lots of experts. But usually little actual experience.

Likewise, job seekers trade stories about a killer résumé or interview trick that landed a friend their dream job. Inevitably though, few have any strategic understanding of the job market. To be fair, few people do.

The key to getting a job is simple. You need to put yourself in the boots of your employer. The odds are, they just want to employ the most personable, most professional, most qualified person for the job, and with the least amount of effort on their part. I want this person to be you! That's why this book focusses on three ideas that many job seeking books do not.

Idea 1: You need to create a presence for yourself

Your *presence* will allow you to tap into jobs more easily. Marketers call this a *personal brand*. The Kardashians and Oprah are two extreme examples. Your *presence* need only be a micro-brand. One that will make you just famous enough to turn an otherwise cold-call on an employer (think telemarketers at mealtime) into a warm-call (think coffee with a new friend).

Whether they like the idea or not, everybody has a personal brand. *Lazy, party-animal, angry, spiteful...* are not desirable ones to an employer. Better ones might be *intelligent, hard working, professional, personable...*

Your *presence* that we'll build together is everything about yourself that will make you the ideal candidate for your new job. It's what will give an employer the confidence to employ you. It's the research that you've done to understand your new job. It's your LinkedIn profile, informed by your research, that an employer can discreetly look at to find out more about you. It's the professionalism and confidence, underpinned by your job research, that you radiate when you're networking.

Idea 2: The focus of a job application should always be on the employer

A résumé is not all about you! The key is to understand that a résumé is a personal marketing document that's all about making the job of employing you an easy one. When you think of your résumé in those terms it becomes obvious what should go in, what should stay out, and what should be emphasized.

By the time the foundations of your *presence* are in place, it's possible that you will have already met the person who will employ you. That will allow you to write a laser focused job application to someone you already have a relationship with...a friendly, personable, professional résumé and cover letter that address all of a job's selection criteria, and conveys your confidence that you're qualified for the job you're applying for.

Idea 3: Technology has changed the way the job market works

Some aspects of job seeking haven't changed. Others have, even compared to a decade ago.

Networks have always been important, as have résumés and cover letters. However, to the inexperienced job seeker, the emphasis on résumés and cover letters is greater than ever. That's because the recruitment industry's tool kit has changed. It's now common for recruiters to use Applicant Tracking Software (ATS) to compare hundreds of applications to a job description, automatically rank them, and so help to quickly create a shortlist of applicants to interview. This new efficiency is why recruiting sites are always saying *send your résumé* or *apply online.*

Résumés are tangible, so the media, family and friends, and the education system focus on them. This leaves many graduates with the false impression that getting a job is *solely* reliant on having a perfect résumé. That in turn leads to the silver bullet approach to job seeking – submitting the same carefully constructed résumé to every job they see advertised. It's a trap that's less likely to be successful because a résumé needs to be tailored for each job, and because of the 80/20 rule of job seeking (four in five jobs are not advertised).

Too many graduates ignore the 80/20 rule and spend too much effort competing for the 20% pool of jobs. Sure, there'll always be advertised jobs that are worth applying for, but wouldn't it be more sensible to spend 20% of your effort on the 20% of the jobs that are advertised, and 80% of your effort on the 80% of jobs that aren't?

Here's the bit that's changed in the job seeker's favor. Although you still access unadvertised jobs through networking just like old-timers did, there's a new generation of tools at your disposal to find and research those jobs – Google, LinkedIn and jobscan. They're what I teach you to harness in this book. If you use them properly, you'll have a better chance of creating laser focused job applications, often for hiring managers you already know.

Throughout this book I deliberately use the pronouns *you* and *your*. That's because *you* need to take responsibility for *your* job research, for *your* LinkedIn profile, for *your* networking, and for *your* job applications.

If you don't tell people what you can do, how on earth are they meant to find out!

Expect my approach to *presence* building and job application writing to be challenging. Embracing challenges is one way we grow both personally and professionally. The research, preparation and practice you'll be doing will help you to move beyond the fear of, and reluctance to, talk about yourself. It will give you the confidence to talk to people about yourself in a way that's meaningful to them, and natural to you. It's important to be able to talk about yourself because if you don't tell other people what you can do, how on earth are they meant to find out!

My approach is not just challenging. It also involves work. But, in contrast to the soul-destroying technique of applying unsuccessfully for sometimes hundreds of jobs, it is empowering because it also sets a foundation for maintaining and building your career once it's under way.

It is about understanding that your résumé needs to be tailored to the job that you're applying for. And it needs to address every point in a job's description. Generic résumés aren't enough. A résumé that demonstrates an understanding of the job the sector it is within, and a hiring manager's problems, hopes and dreams, is far more likely to succeed.

When I started my consulting business, I struggled to get work until I worked that out. Things turned around when my tender responses became more focused. My tenders often took a week or more to write. But, as will be the case for your job applications, after doing that initial lump of work, my next response took only a fraction of the time.

It's understandable that graduates, especially those who have been juggling work and study for many years, will expect to be rewarded with a queue of employers offering them a job. That's rarely the case. A year after graduating, a friend once commented how useful his PhD was. He joked that *it's given me the opportunity to wait tables, work bars, and cart furniture*. His experience is a common one, so don't feel bad if this happens to you.

Nobody can guarantee you instant job search success. But, I can promise you that in a world where four in five jobs are not advertised, you are more likely to have success making warm calls to an employer who already knows you, than competing with everyone else for the 1 in 5 jobs that are advertised.

If you'll allow me, I'd like to help you be the best at job search that you can be. Read on and I'll show you a way to improve your chances of getting the job you want, with an employer you'll enjoy working for, sooner than you might otherwise do.

A note on the FREE companion website

All figures, tables, PowerPoint templates, worksheets and other resources can be downloaded using the QR codes and links in the appendix. These and 4 hours of video tuition are free. If you choose to enter your email address ...

1. I will email you the link to a resources page, from which you can access all the book's resources, and

2. I will notify you when I update the website with new videos and downloads.

Some useful terms

Before we start, here's some terms that I use throughout the book.

Applicant Tracking Software (ATS): Software that some employers use to compare a job application to a job description, and then automatically produce a shortlist of applicants.

Avatar: I show you how to use avatars to document the problems, hopes and dreams of a hiring manager and their workplace. It's a tool we'll use to give you focus when you're creating your LinkedIn profile and your job applications. Also called a persona.

Hiring manager: The person, who, in your new workplace, would be your immediate boss.

Keyword: These are words that people are searching for on LinkedIn. Important keywords relate to job titles and software tools. For example, software engineer, accountant, Excel, Python, Xero...

Presence: This is my version of a personal brand for graduate job seekers. By graduating up the levels of your *presence pyramid,* the idea is to make you just famous enough to find yourself on a hiring manager's radar.

The characters:
- **Alex:** Job seeking graduate.
- **Lou:** Alex's hiring manager.

Introduction

You need to be *proactive* when you're searching for a job. Not *reactive*! By that I mean that you need to reframe the idea of *applying* for a job into *searching* for a job. A résumé always has been, and always will be important. But it's not the silver bullet for getting a job. The way you use a résumé for job search is not straight forward like it once was. As has always been the case, a résumé will work much more effectively if you already have a relationship with an employer.

You need to reframe the idea of applying for a job into searching for a job.

You build relationships with employers by networking. For networking to be effective, you need to have substance. To gain substance, you need to take the time and effort to build the foundations of your presence. It can be a lot of work. But if you're out of work, your job is to get a job. That means long days of researching and reflecting. Not long days on social media and then working on job search with the time that's left over! Sending texts, checking email, time on social media, and doing laundry does not move you closer to getting a job! Your ability to curb your nonproductive time is a test for how well you work unsupervised – an important workplace requirement these days.

Everybody wants the silver bullet for getting a job. That one thing that will set them apart from their competition. The perfect résumé layout. The perfect email subject line. The perfect email signoff. Ask 10 different people their opinion on what the silver bullet is, and you'll be sure to get 10 different answers. My opinion makes that 11! The truth is that the silver bullet for getting your job is buried in the following story.

> *In the 1950s, piano maestro Arthur Rubenstein was walking along a New York street when a stranger asked him "can you tell me how to get to Carnegie Hall?" His answer..."practice, practice, practice".*

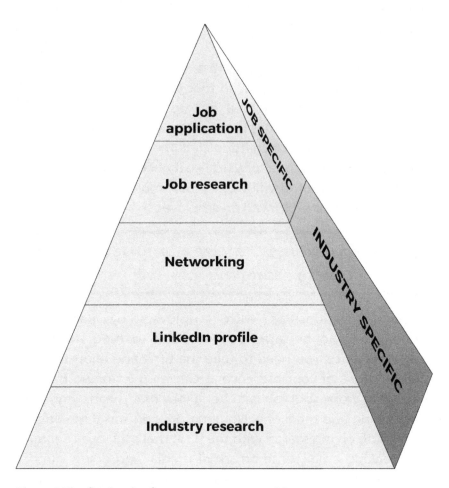

Figure 1: The five levels of your presence pyramid.

Whether the story is true or not is unimportant. But, the idea behind it is. To get a job, you need to be prepared to work, work, work!

The work I think you need to do is summarized as my 5 level *presence pyramid* (Figure 1). The knowledge and skills you gain by completing each level support the tasks you need to do at the next higher level. In level 1 you research your industry, and that helps you fill in your LinkedIn profile in level 2. Having a good LinkedIn profile makes you more confident in networking situations in level 3, and because it's a living document, the things you learn while networking feed back into your LinkedIn profile. Over time, your LinkedIn profile improves and becomes a place where you're proud to send friends, family and potential employers so they can discreetly find out more about you.

By the time you find a job to apply for, the lion's share of writing your job application is done. Your job application is the peak of the pyramid (level 5). It will be a version of your LinkedIn profile you created in level 2, that's been edited to have focus on the job that you're applying for (level 4). That's a much smaller task than writing a job application from scratch.

Each level of your *presence pyramid* involves work that's comparable in effort to a college assignment. The higher you climb your *presence pyramid*, the more refined your *presence* will become.

Your *presence* is an important tool for your job search. It's everything about you that an employer sees. The depth of research embodied in it can mean the difference between a cold call (telemarketer at mealtime) and a warm call (coffee with a new friend). The more committed you are to working on your *presence pyramid*, the more likely you are to craft your *presence* in a way that leaves an employer in no doubt that you are professional, committed, and a good employee choice.

This book has four parts

This book is written in four parts. In part one I talk about the 2020s job market, and how and why its different to the job market even a few years ago. In part two, I show you how to focus your job research on an industry. In part three, I show you how to build on the research you did in part two, and give it focus on the job that you're applying for. In part four I present worked examples of advertised jobs and the research, LinkedIn profile, résumé and cover letter that address them.

PART 1: Context for the 2020s job market

In part one I set the context for job search in the 2020s. Technical advancements combined with fallout from the 2008 GFC created the perfect storm for change in the way that both employers and job seekers approached the job market.

Covid triggered a recession of GFC scale. This time the driver was a health crisis rather than a flakey financial system, so expect the bounce back and long-term impacts to take a different form. The most significant long-term impact of covid on the job market will be the rearrangement of where jobs are, including the return of some manufacturing from overseas. That has implications, not only for the types of skills that the job market needs, but also for how you frame your job applications. On top of covid, the decarbonization of the energy sector is going to create even more manufacturing jobs.

Following that discussion, I ask you to imagine that you're an employer. By asking yourself *if I was an employer, what would I want from an employee*, you'll gain some insights into why employing someone is such a big deal, especially for small business. You'll learn that there's a big incentive for employers to employ the right person. When you put yourself in an employer's boots, it becomes clear that your job is to make their job of employing you an easy one.

PART 2: Laying the foundation for getting a job

In part two I'll introduce you to the first three levels of your *presence pyramid* (Figure 1). Your *industry research* informs what you put in your LinkedIn profile and how you express it. Researching your industry and creating a *LinkedIn profile* that's informed by that research, will allow you to be more effective and confident at *networking, relationship building and informational interviewing*.

Notice that the pyramid has a wide foundation, and gains focus as you move towards the top. Creating your *presence* does not need to be an extravagant exercise, but it does need to be considered and thorough.

PRESENCE PYRAMID LEVEL 1 – Industry research

The foundation of your *presence pyramid* is research on the job you want to do within the industry you want to do it in. Every type of job gains focus when you add an industry layer. For example, if you want to work as an administrator, then your research would reveal that administrating different types of offices (e.g. legal versus medical) requires different skills.

Your research should uncover the expectations (training, working hours, etc) that your industry has on its employees. With that knowledge, you need to decide whether or not those expectations align with yours. Prepare to discover that your first career choice might not be for you.

An important tool to fall out of your industry research are the avatar graphics that we'll craft. These are fictional characterizations of your new hiring manager's and new workplace's key attributes. Creating these will take work. But it will be time well spent. You'll be rewarded with a useful tool that will help you characterize your new hiring manager and workplace in a way that's easy to digest, so you can more easily write laser targeted job applications.

The industry research and self-reflection you do in level 1 will also inform both what you include in your LinkedIn profile, and the way you express yourself in it. It will also help you identify gaps in your knowledge that you need to close through additional education. I'll point you to some websites (some free, others affordable) that are ideal for that.

PRESENCE PYRAMID LEVEL 2 – LinkedIn profile

LinkedIn is best described as a website for people with professional attitudes. It's not just for people who have been to university or college. These days people in hospitality and trades are just as likely to be as professional as someone in engineering or law.

I talk about LinkedIn as being like a three legged stool – completed profile, maintained profile, and relationship building. Lose one leg and the stool falls over.

Your LinkedIn profile should reflect your industry research, and how you see yourself fit into your chosen industry. Think of it as your personal webpage that's dedicated to your professional life. I'll show you how to improve your chances of people finding your profile via LinkedIn search and LinkedIn recommendations. Other times you will refer people to it.

PRESENCE PYRAMID LEVEL 3 – Networking and relationship building

For many people, the word *networking* implies the deliberate building of transactional relationships (ie. only wanting to meet someone because they might give you a job). A better way to think of networking is *relationship building.* The simple act of building relationships at a networking event.

Networking is a bit like sport and music. The more you practice it, the better you get. Don't expect to be good at it to start with. Few people are. The good news is that few people expect you to be when you start out. With practice, you'll find your networking "voice".

However you prefer to think of it, networking can happen anywhere at any time. Your industry research and your LinkedIn profile will help you be more confident and effective in networking situations.

Relationships are important because most jobs are not advertised. Some of the people you meet will be important to your job search, others will advise you, others will introduce you to people who will become important to your job search, and others will just be pleasant to chat to. But you never know! The famous French microbiologist Louis Pasteur (the inventor of pasteurization) is quoted as saying *"...chance favors only the prepared mind".*[1] In the context of job search, that means that in the absence of research, it can be hard to recognize a job opportunity when it presents itself. So, if you're prepared, sometimes opportunities arise from unlikely situations.

"...chance favors only the prepared mind.

By making a commitment to relationship building, you'll increase the odds of creating situations where you can make warm calls to industry people who can advise and help you. Calls where you and the person you're calling on already know each other.

---

1   Louise Pasteur, 1854, Lecture at the University of Lille

PART 3: Applying for a job

In part three I introduce you to the *job research* and *job application* levels of your *presence pyramid* (Figure 1). Too many people do a bad job of their job applications.

PRESENCE PYRAMID LEVEL 4 – Job research

You move to the job research level when you've identified a job opportunity. The work you've done in the bottom three levels of your *presence pyramid* should make this level easy. Job research is all about giving your industry research focus, and then applying it to a job opportunity. You'll take the avatars you created for your industry research and customize them to the job you're applying for.

PRESENCE PYRAMID LEVEL 5 – Job application

In this section we'll talk about both the art and the science of writing cover letters and résumés. Every job application you write must be laser focused on your job specific avatars, as well as every detail of the job description and job selection criteria. That way you'll demonstrate your depth of understanding, not only of the job you're applying for, but also the workplace that's advertising the job.

PART 4: Examples of job applications

I begin part four with a quick recap of how to go about researching to find information about your new job and the workplace its within. Then I provide you with three examples of job advertisements, and worked examples showing you how to apply for them. I show you the avatars you'd create, your LinkedIn profile that's informed by your avatars, and how your LinkedIn profile gets copied and modified to form the foundation of your résumé and your cover letter.

PART ONE – Context for the 2020s jobs market

The covid recession blew shockwaves into the job market. Throughout history, pandemics, wars, disasters, depressions and recessions have come and gone. In their aftermath, there's always a period of rebuilding, followed by a new normal. The 2008 Global Financial Crisis (GFC) triggered changes in the way the job market worked. Expect that covid will trigger changes in what types of jobs are available, where they are, and the skillsets that will be needed to do them.

Many older job search books focus on applying for jobs with large employers and assume that all employers fill positions in the same way. That is no longer true. Technical advances combined with fallout from the GFC, created the perfect storm for change in the way that both employers and job seekers approached the job market. That means that you should view the job search advice you get from anyone who does not have recent (successful) job search experience with caution.

These days there are many ways employers go about employing people.

- Some employers like to (or are obliged to) advertise jobs, and others are not.
- Some employers use Applicant Tracking Software (ATS) to automatically shortlist applicants, and others don't.
- Some employers have HR staff whose job it is to employ people, and others don't.

The good news is that most jobs are not advertised. And, when their workplace policies allow them to, most employers prefer to fill their positions informally.

Employers looked at résumés differently after the GFC

For Richard Bolles[2] the 2008 GFC was a turning point. Many businesses went broke. For those businesses that remained, when they advertised a job, both the volume of applications and the number of high quality applicants increased. That provided an environment where employers could change the way they filled positions. They could suddenly take their pick of any number of high quality applicants. The result was a shift towards a more economical approach to employing people – short term project-based jobs at the expense of full time jobs.

As well, whenever possible, jobs were reimagined and deskilled. During the GFC and in the months following, the dip in job creation[3] provided the opportunity for employers to do this. Employees and unions in an insecure job market were not inclined to complain about this structural change as much as they would in more prosperous times.

Job growth mirrors population growth so there are always new jobs

After its recovery from the 2008 GFC, the US consistently added around 170,000 jobs most months regardless of who was in power.

In two decades (one before and one after the GFC), on average, western populations grew by 18.9% (21% in the US).[4] Along with population growth came job growth. After its recovery from the 2008 GFC and prior to the covid shock, the US consistently added around 170,000 jobs most months regardless of who was in power[5]. In English speaking western countries, post GFC

---

2   Richard Bolles, 2019, What Color Is Your Parachute? 2020: A Practical Manual for Job-Hunters and Career-Changers, Ten Speed Press, Chapter 1.

3   Steve Benen, January 2020, Job growth cooled a little as 2019 came to a close, https://www.msnbc.com/rachel-maddow-show/job-growth-cooled-little-2019-came-close-n1116251

4   Our World In Data, 2021, https://www.ourworldindata.org/grapher/population?time=1997..2019&country=AUS+GBR+USA+CAN+NZL

5   Steve Benen, January 2020, loc. cit.

---

unemployment rates fell consistently, and then remained stable until covid in early 2020.[6] All their populations were increasing on a similar trajectory, so I think it's safe to assume that a similar job creation story existed in all Western countries prior to covid.

> *Some people are unemployed simply because they haven't been taught how to look for work.*

So why, when post GFC thru pre-covid (2009–2020) statistics showed that there were around 170,000 jobs created each month in the US (regardless of who was in power), did we mostly hear how hard it was to get a job? What if, aside from the cohort of chronically unemployed people that exists in every community, there's another group of job seekers, who are unsuccessful, at least in part, because they are not good at job seeking?

You've probably heard the old saying that goes *Lies, damned lies and statistics*. I think that there's over-reporting of job seekers not being able to get work, and under reporting of success stories. And that makes the idea of an unemployment crisis misleading. On the one hand, the media, reporting on unemployment, naturally seek out unemployed people to speak to. On the other hand, people who are good at job seeking are too busy to comment because they're knuckling down in their new jobs!

The job market changed after the 2008 GFC

The GFC and technology advances that were maturing around that time combined to create the perfect storm for job market change (Table 1). Internet capacity and speed improved and the internet "cloud" gained traction. Home computing became more functional, user friendly and faster. Smartphones emerged. Job lift-outs in newspapers were mostly replaced by recruitment websites. Forms on websites became easy to access and easy to fill

---

6   International Labour Organization, ILOSTAT database (June 21, 2020), Unemployment, total (% of total labor force) (modeled ILO estimate) – Australia, United States, Canada, United Kingdom, New Zealand https://www.data.worldbank.org/indicator/ SL.UEM.TOTL.ZS?end=2020&locations=AU-US-CA-GB-NZ&start=2008&view=chart

---

in, and so jobs became easy for employers to advertise, and, fueled by email, easy to apply for. Applicant Tracking Software (ATS) that automatically shortlist job applicants by comparing their résumé to a job's description emerged. And because the web had a greater geographical reach than print advertising, each job was exposed to more potential applicants.

LinkedIn and big data (huge employment databases) added another layer of complexity to the job market. Suddenly, if you wanted to gain exposure to the automated opportunities offered by recruitment agencies and online job sites, you also needed to present your information so that web robots could easily make sense of your online résumé and LinkedIn profile.

The role of résumés changed. Many employers began to use Applicant Tracking Software (ATS), so humans no longer looked at every résumé sent to them. In contrast, smaller employers without access to ATS were left to manually wade through the huge numbers of résumés they now received in response to the new generation of super-effective job advertisements, and super-easy methods of applying for jobs.

Table 1: Changes to the job market since the GFC.

ITEM	PRE 2008 GFC	POST 2008 GFC
Advertising	Large weekly job lift-outs in local newspapers.	Small weekly job sections in local newspapers, if at all. Job seekers notified by email the moment a suitable job appears.
	Restricted to the delivery area of newspaper.	No geographical limitations, so ads get seen by more people.
	Newspaper ads are cumbersome to organize and subject to print deadlines.	Mostly ads on recruitment websites that are simple for employers and job seekers to use, and not subject to print deadlines.
Responding to ads	Mostly by post.	Mostly by email or online forms.
	Individual résumés and cover letters need to be addressed, printed, signed and posted.	Quick and easy turn around. Cut, paste, modify address and job title, and then email the application. Applicants can apply for more jobs more easily.
	Your résumé was the main way for employers to find out information about you	Your LinkedIn profile needs to be completed and up-to-date, and easy for web robots to harvest. Shortlisted applicant's LinkedIn (and social media profiles) may be viewed.
Evaluating applications	You only need to format your résumé so that it is easy for an employer/recruiter to read.	Your résumé also needs to be easy for Applicant Tracking Software (ATS) to analyze it. Even if ATS is used, layout is still important if your résumé is shortlisted for human review.
	Employers manually review all résumés.	Due to more effective advertising and email, employers are faced with a mountain of applications for each position. Some employers use ATS to automatically create a shortlist of applicants. Small employers must process responses manually. Sometimes there are hundreds.

Make the new job market work for you

Here's the good news. Rather than the growth in population creating increased competition for jobs, and the changes in ways the job market operates (Table 1) presenting a hurdle for job seekers, they present an opportunity. That's because many employers are overwhelmed by the recruiting process and would kill to stumble across a good candidate without having to engage in it. But to harness that opportunity, you need to be willing to reimagine the way you go about searching for a job.

Your reimagined job search involves aligning your *presence pyramid* (Figure 1) with the job you are applying for, ensuring that your application addresses the job selection criteria, having a LinkedIn profile that reinforces and expands on what you've written in your résumé, and just getting out there! Some people call that *hustling*.

If you're applying for a job with a large employer, you need to leap their Applicant Tracking Software (ATS) hurdle. You do that by formatting your résumé so the ATS can analyze it (and sometimes by harnessing relationships you have with people in that workplace). Just understanding how ATS works can give you an edge over other applicants. ATS are not a bad thing. They impose a layer of rigor that forces you to format your résumé in a way that makes it easy for recruiters to evaluate.

And, by the way, ATS pay no attention to the visual design of your résumé and its fonts! In fact, fancy formatting can work against you. I'll show you ATS friendly formatting when I talk about résumé writing in part 3.

Expect employers who don't have access to ATS to be overwhelmed by having to manually wade through hundreds of résumés. There are as many ways to approach the manual evaluation of job applications as there are employers. Most aim for a pile of 10 or so applications to study in detail. From the pile of 10 they'll aim to pick three or four people to interview. Some only look at the first 10 applications in the order they receive them. Others aim to choose 10 within a set time. Others have a quick look at every résumé and pick the 10 that jump out at them.

Table 2: Five ways small and large employers recruit staff.

		RECRUITING METHOD	COMMENTS
More common for small business		1. Networking and recommendations.	Networking at industry events. Recommendations from friends, friends-of-friends, teachers, local community.
		2. Small jobs that turn into bigger opportunities.	Employers often test people out. If you prove to be a good worker then they magically find more work.
		3. Advertised jobs that are evaluated directly by an employer.	This is cold calling by invitation. Employers have no way of knowing anything about you beyond your job application. In your application, it's important to make it easy for them to employ you by addressing every item in the job description, and inserting links to your LinkedIn profile and other relevant web *presence*.
More common for large business		4. Advertised jobs that are evaluated directly by a human resources specialist within a company. Some companies use ATS.	Cover letters are important for some job applications and not others. It's important for you to address all the selection criteria in your application. ATS will have a better chance of shortlisting you if you do this right. A human should be able to add your application to a yes-pile in <30 seconds. Links to your LinkedIn profile and your other relevant web *presence* become important once you're short-listed.
		5. Advertised jobs that are funneled through a recruiting agency. Most agencies use ATS.	

Table 2 summarizes the five main ways that employers use to recruit staff. Although your LinkedIn profile and your résumé are important for each, your résumé's role in the job application process will often differ depending on the size of the business. Your LinkedIn profile becomes more important the closer you get to being short listed (sometimes more important than a résumé for rows 1–2 in Table 2).

Some employers (rows 1–2 in Table 2) prefer not to advertise jobs. Friends of friends, networking, online forums, and LinkedIn are their preferred ways of finding staff. It's important to make it easy for this group of employers to discreetly look you up on LinkedIn.

Sometimes a hiring manager will shortlist you without you realizing it. That means that you may not be competing with a big group of candidates. In other words, if you miss out on the job, it's because you're just not the right fit for the business.

If a hiring manager does look you up on LinkedIn, there should be something there for them to look at. Don't drop your guard! Even if you think you're on a sure thing, you're not! The quality of your résumé and LinkedIn profile is still important, and can make the difference between being hired or not. Their quality (or lack of) can also affect your starting wage.

Relationships improve your chances no matter what the size of the business. They can work in subtle ways. For example, a hiring manager might call HR and say something like *I met Alex Johnson at an event recently. Impressive graduate! Please be sure to include Alex's application in the shortlist.*

Where a job is advertised (rows 3–5 in Table 2), the better you address the job selection criteria in your application, the more likely you are to be short listed. More on that in part 3 and part 4.

The workplace will change post covid

People who think that the 2008 GFC can be compared to the 2020s covid pandemic are wrong! They are not directly comparable because the GFC was a financial crisis and covid is a health crisis. Governments learnt lessons from the GFC, and for the most part, the economic environment that led to the

GFC no longer exists. Financial institutions are more secure than ever because they now operate under highly regulated lending, funding and reporting regimes.

My point is that we can expect the recovery from covid to take a different form than that of the GFC. As I do my final review of this book (March 2022), the world is in a state of discombobulation. It looks like the covid pandemic will end, but nobody can be sure exactly what form the recovery will take. That said, some possibilities are beginning to emerge.

Like the GFC did, covid has caused massive disruption and sudden unemployment. Many businesses have failed. Of those that have survived, as was the case after the GFC, many will embrace the opportunity to reduce costs.

For employers, labor costs were a big saving that fell out of the GFC. Rent costs will be the big saving that falls out of covid. It is now common for remote working employees provide their own office space. Many of the other changes to the job market will be based on the geography of where work is done.

As much as covid has been responsible for massive unemployment in some sectors, its also been responsible for massive growth in others. Workforce restructuring will continue. Both where work is done, and the type of work that is done there will change.

There will be employment opportunities as supply chain resilience and supply chain security becomes more important in the minds of both business and government. Countries around the world have already begun to bring some of their manufacturing back onshore. The economics of swapping cheap overseas labor with technology, particularly robotization, are beginning to stack up for some industries.

I predict that we'll look back on the 2020s as being a period of workforce rearrangement and change. Some of the changes have implications for the skillsets that you'll need to make you employable. Expect more local manufacturing of some goods, less commuting and business travel, the rearrangement of services (office supplies, café's, etc) to reflect where work is now being done, and more online retail at the expense of brick-and-mortar retail.

Office work: More work will be done "flex"
Summary: More people will work from home. Knowledge of cloud software and a demonstratable ability to work independently will be required.

Covid has tested infrastructures that were in place but not being fully used. Infrastructure like high-speed internet, videoconferencing, and the internet cloud. The crisis has forced business to undertake a real-life experiment. It has educated them in a new way of doing things, and for many it has worked out.

Post pandemic, some businesses will make a move towards leaner and more flexible office arrangements. Fixed costs like office space will come into focus. Why have a desk for every person when much of your workforce can work efficiently and happily from home? It's not uncommon for office rents to be $10,000 or more per desk space per year[7], so a reduction in the need to rent city office space could translate to a big saving for a business' bottom line.

Other scenarios include less crowded offices, and hot-desking accompanied by more rigorous cleaning and disinfecting regimes.

Some office workers are thriving in the changed geography of work and others are not. Working from home has improved the quality of life for many people. Those who are enjoying the extra time with family, and spending less money on commuting and grooming, will resist going back to working the old way.

In the end, a new office work environment will emerge from a combination of some employer's desire to conduct business effectively while reducing overheads, and some employees desire for a better work life balance. Some businesses will embrace this change quickly and attract staff who like to work that way. Businesses that are slow to change will be less competitive if they continue to pay high

---

7 My web research indicates that inner city office rental is around $80 / m2 / month. A common office space allowance for an employee is 10 m2 ($800/month). So a company with 100 employees could be paying $1 million a year rental.

---

rents, and will either attract workers who like the office environment, or they even may find it difficult to compete for staff.

Ben Chestnut of MailChimp says his 1200 employees do not want things to go all the way back to normal. MailChimp's hybrid approach is called *flex*. So that MailChimp can make space planning decisions, staff must commit to being primarily in the office or primarily at home. Ben thinks MailChimp is still going to need physical space. He thinks that people will do their deep thought work at home, and that they'll get together sometimes so they can more easily brainstorm, collaborate and socialize.[8]

There is no one answer to how the post pandemic workplace will look because some employers are naturally trusting and others naturally suspicious, some employees are naturally trustworthy and others are naturally untrustworthy, and some people like to work from home and others don't.

The best way for you to navigate this period of the uncertain workplace is to develop good work practices so that you can demonstrate that you can work independently. If you are a recent graduate, even your success in self managing online study is a clue for employers that you can do that.

Ideally, you'll have the infrastructure (fast internet, computer and workspace) that would allow you to work remotely. And you'll know how to use the cloud software that being used by an employer.

Manufacturing: The sector will grow and require more technical skills.
Summary: Some manufacturing will return from overseas. There will be jobs constructing and fitting out the new manufacturing plants and in logistics. To be competitive, the new plants will embrace robotics and so will require a more qualified workforce. As well, decarbonization will cause massive growth in the clean energy sector.

In the last couple of decades, advances in the internet and in logistics has facilitated the movement of many manufacturing

8   Guy Raz, July 12, 2021, How I Built This, Mailchimp: Ben Chestnut
      https://www.npr.org/2021/07/09/1014699766/mailchimp-ben-chestnut

jobs to countries where lower wages and environmental standards meant that goods could be produced cheaply. Many goods are designed in one country and then manufactured in another.

The sudden onset of the covid pandemic caught many businesses and governments off guard and has made them aware just how fragile some aspects of globalization have made them. Initially there were shortages of medical supplies and an inability to manufacture them locally. Even the best supply chains and logistics could not overcome closed borders and the skullduggery that occurred early on for covid medical equipment. It's not just medical equipment that's affected. As an example, in many places, water treatment chemicals are sourced from overseas. Clean water is the foundation for community health. A hiccup in the supply chain of those had the potential to add a gastro illness layer of stress onto an already pandemic-stretched health system.

You can't 'politic' your way out of health or environmental crises, so expect governments to take (at least a little) more notice of their science and national security advisors in the future. Many country's supply chains are not resilient. And so the debate about having multiple sources of supply and the re-industrialization of some nations begins![9]

Expect that governments will fine tune their versions of globalization. They may insist that some manufacturing and services be brought back from overseas. Some businesses will make the decision do that anyhow. Those manufacturers that do come back onshore, will tend to invest in the latest software and equipment (robotics and 3D printing wherever possible). Robots will replace cheap overseas labor (and in some places expensive overseas labor). Called *onshoring* and *reshoring*, its already happening in Australia[10] and America...

---

9   Gareth Hutchens, May 3 2020, Coronavirus is focusing attention on how fragile global supply chains can be, so how will Australia respond?, https://www.abc.net.au/news/2020-05-03/coronavirus-global-supply-chains-and-essential-services-exposed/12209246

10   Peter Roberts, Onshoring and reshoring is real says circuitwise, September 28 2020, https://www.aumanufacturing.com.au/onshoring-and-reshoring-is-real-says-circuitwise

---

Of the 746 manufacturing companies surveyed in May and June of 2020, 69% are looking to bring production back to North America, 38% are actively hiring, and 55% said they are likely to invest in automation...[11]

There will be new jobs designing and building the new machinery, retrofitting old premises, and in building new premises to house them. There will also be a demand for highly skilled labor to operate the machinery and manage production. And it goes without saying that there'll be a requirement for more logistics and support staff to support the increased local production.

The highly evolved pre-covid logistics that enabled a separation of business functions on an international scale (head office, design, and manufacture, often in different countries), may translate into similar separations but at national and regional scales. The side-effects of more people working from home (less road, rail and airport congestion), may also act to further improve the efficiency of logistics.

On top of onshoring, governments around the world are decarbonizing. Fossil fuel companies are on-the-nose. Pension funds and other investors are selling their stock. And for reasons relating to consumer pressure and risk governance, banks are less likely to fund them. Renewables are the new golden child. The sector is being increasingly backed by government policy and lenders. Watch this space!

Hospitality: There'll be a mix of shrinkage, relocation and reimagination.
Summary: Reduced tourist and business travel may lead to a decline in the entire sector. There'll be an increased demand for café's closer to workers homes.

The way people holiday and do business may change, at least until covid is a less threatening disease and consumer confidence returns.

---

11 Stephanie Neil, March 8 2021, How Automation Enables Viable Reshoring, https://www.automationworld.com/factory/workforce/article/21307149/how-automation-enables-viable-reshoring

---

International tourism and business travel will decline in the short/medium term due to tight border control and traveler anxiety. Anxiety relates not only to contracting covid, but also to the prospect of getting stuck without travel insurance if another pandemic emerges.

Covid has had a huge impact on the cruise ship industry. Although the industry generated $55.5 billion of economic activity and 436,000+ jobs in the US in 2019,[12] Carnival Cruises has brought forward the retirement of eighteen cruise ships, an indication that that industry will continue to suffer.[13] Airlines are also bringing forward the retirement of many aircraft.[14]

At a more practical level, with a reduction in company income, for some businesses the money to pay for travel simply may not be there. Just today, a friend commented that the covid lockdowns have forced his interstate clients to adopt video conferencing in place of face to face visits. He is hoping that post covid, this new way of doing business will add to his bottom line, and improve his lifestyle. He wants the regular online meetings to continue, and be supported by less frequent face to face visits. The new normal for many businesses perhaps?

Some hospitality jobs will move closer to where workers live rather than where they used to commute to. Food services that move from high rent inner city locations to lower rent larger footprint suburban locations may take the opportunity to reimagine and expand their offering. Local cafés will be busier because more people will be working from home.

12 BREA press release, November 19 2020, Cruise Industry Contribution to U.S. Economy Grew to $55.5 Billion in 2019, Generating More Than 436,000 American Jobs (USA), Cruise line international association, November 17, 2020, https://www.cruising.org/en/news-and-research/press-room/2020/november/cruise-industry-contribution-to-us-economy-grew-to-55-billion-in-2019

13 Staff writer, October 6 2020, Cruise ships and covid: Incredible photos show giant cruise ships being scrapped, https://www.traveller.com.au/cruise-ships-and-covid19-incredible-photos-show-giant-cruise-ships-being-scrapped-h1r7kw

14 Thomas Pallini, May 22 2020, Even more iconic planes are disappearing from the sky earlier than planned as the coronavirus continues to wreak airline havoc, Business Insider, https://www.businessinsider.com.au/coronavirus-havoc-forces-airlines-to-retire-iconic-planes-sooner-2020-3

Retail: Brick and mortar will shrink. Online will grow.

Summary: Smaller retail footprint. Focus on online shopping.

Retail has always struggled in the face of high rents. Cash flow sensitive retailers will fold, particularly those who cannot meet their lease obligations. Others will return with a smaller footprint. It will be another blow if a social distancing culture emerges with consumers.

Some retail workers will need to find their place in the online environment. It is even possible that retail stores might become showrooms for online stores.[15]

Summing up the post covid workplace

The take-home is that from now on, when you're looking for work, many things will not be how they were before the pandemic. When you're applying for a job, you'll need to demonstrate that you can work in both the covid and hopefully, post covid world. You need to be on top of your game!

One thing is for sure, in a high unemployment environment, sending a volley of unsolicited emails with your résumé as an attachment is doomed to fail. You'll occasionally read success stories about people who use this technique. Typically, embedded in the article is advice along the lines of *you've just got to keep sending off your résumé.* The press also like to publish stories about lotto winners! You should not feel encouraged by either of these stories. News outlets publish them because they know that readers will click on them. They are misleading stories about luck and exceptions. Not norms.

Even with a gold standard application, winning an advertised job can be tough. In such an environment, your *presence* and your ability to network are your friends. More on those in part two of this book. But for now, I want to expand a bit on how employers think. That will give you context for how you need to go about presenting yourself as an ideal employee.

---

15 Erik Norland, 27/4/2020, How covid pandemic could reshape consumer and business behavior, https://www.globaltimes.cn/content/1186947.shtml

---

Imagine you're the person evaluating your job application

When you're applying for jobs, it's easy to see rejection only from your perspective. Take a moment to do that. Take a deep breath. Now imagine that you're the person who's tasked with evaluating your job application, and a hundred or more others.

Unless they are a human resources specialist, the person hiring you (the *hiring manager*) is unlikely to enjoy hiring people. It just creates extra work for them and takes them away from their productive day-to-day work. It starts with an enormous time commitment to write your job description, advertise, shortlist, and interview. Then come the administrative tasks that are associated with employing you. Then training you for your role in the company. Training also takes resources away from productive work. It's a double whammy – less work getting done by the trainer while paying a trainee who's unproductive. Then there's risk. More on that in the next section.

So, the key to writing a good job application is to imagine that you're the person who is evaluating it. In different workplaces this person will have different pressures on them. That means you need to understand your hiring manager's pain points and consider what you, if you were to be their employee, could do to ease them.

Always try to reduce the friction for employing you

Always try to reduce the friction for employing you. Employers want to employ you, but you need to make that decision an easy one for them. You need to respect their time. If you're responding to an advertisement, they're probably under pressure to reduce a pile of one hundred or more applications to a short list of people to interview.

Are you starting to understand why it is not okay to download a résumé template from the web, change a few names and dates, modify it to reflect you, and then send it off?

Why employing someone is a risk for small business

In these days of risk averse decision making, you need to ensure that your job application stands on its own merits. Risk means different things to the different people who might be involved in hiring you. Agency recruiters risk their placement fee if you don't work out. Internal recruiters need to be able to defend their decision to their seniors. Small employers risk their business if they employ the wrong person. And, once you've been hired, there's the financial responsibility of finding your wage, and the financial burden if you turn out to be the wrong person for the job. That's what employers call a bad hire.

There are many ways an employer might measure the cost of a bad hire. How long an employee stays is one measure. Accounting for the cost of recruiting, cost of training (your wages and the wages and lost productivity of the person training you), and time lapse to becoming fully productive, the cost of onboarding new employee can be up to a third of their annual salary.[16]

A friend of mine hired the wrong person. That decision cost him a quarter of a million dollars.

Years ago, a friend employed an American fellow to work in his Hong Kong business. After relocating, accommodating, setting up new offices and employment related expenses, his new staff member had cost him around a quarter million dollars. At the end of the trial period it was clear the new employee was not a good fit and so my friend had to let him go.

Another measure is *bad apples that spoil the bunch*. The slack for an employee not pulling their weight gets taken up by the good employees, who then get burnt out in the process. Morale drops and poor performance spreads like a virus.[17] Bad apples are a double whammy impact on the business when combined with the cost of onboarding.

---

16 John Hall, May 2019, The Cost Of Turnover Can Kill Your Business And Make Things Less Fun, https://www.forbes.com/sites/johnhall/2019/05/09/the-cost-of-turnover-can-kill-your-business-and-make-things-less-fun/#2d50a3f87943

17 Falon Fatimi, September 2016, The True Cost Of A Bad Hire – It's More Than You Think, forbes.com/sites/falonfatemi/2016/09/28/the-true-cost-of-a-bad-hire-its-more-than-you-think/#bc6d5a44aa41 See also ... https://www.inc.com/john-brandon/real-cost-hiring-wrong-employee.html

---

So, there it is. There's a big incentive for employers to employ the right person for the job. There's a lot at stake for them. You're not the only one with skin in the game. As someone applying for a job, you'll fare a lot better if you make your new employer's job easy by giving them the confidence that you're qualified, that you'll stay long enough to make training you worthwhile, and that you won't be a bad apple.

Four reasons why an employer would regret employing you

Every now and then an employer will regret hiring someone. Sometimes someone just turns out to be the wrong fit. Other times it quickly becomes obvious that this new relationship will not survive its honeymoon. Here's some reasons why a reasonable employer might judge they've made a bad hire.

1. Malingerer
Malingerers and employees with bad personal characteristics can make for a dysfunctional workplace. Laziness can be infectious. If left unchecked, everyone's standards can drop.

2. Toxic personality
A toxic personality can make for an unpleasant workplace. There is a danger that good staff might leave.

3. Someone who lied
Don't lie. If you're not qualified in the way that your interview and job application suggests, you'll not only be unproductive, you'll consume time from other workers who would otherwise be productive.

While you can bask in the glory of having tricked someone into employing you, unless you quickly get up to speed, you risk being laid off during your probation period. And, don't fool yourself. Every industry has a community. Communities talk! Engineers hang around engineers. Plumbers hang around plumbers. Health professionals hang around health professionals. I'm sure you get the idea.

The message is, a wrong move with one employer can sometimes make it hard to get a job with another. At its extreme, lying on a résumé can be a criminal offense.[18]

4. Unprofessional behavior

It's important to understand what expectations your employer might have of you. The odds are its someone who can be professional in the workplace. The level of professionalism you display in any job sets you up for respect in your workplace, promotions, and an easier path to your next workplace.

Occupational Health and Safety (OH&S) standards and workplace procedures mean that these days being a *professional* is no longer a category of job. It's a state of being. It's about having high personal standards in a workplace. And that includes the types of behaviors that the #MeToo, the #BLM and other movements have exposed!

Here's some thoughts on what it means to be professional...

- **Supervision:** Employees who can work unsupervised require less management and so cost less to employ.

- **Trust:** Employees who demonstrate they work the hours they're meant to do not consume resources to monitor them.

- **Ambassadors:** Employees who represent a business well, and can be trusted to visit customers. They dress appropriately, have good road manners, don't swear excessively, and treat others with respect and courtesy. They won't be the subject of a customer complaint.

Belinda Fuller's 12 professional behavior tips amount to giving your best at all times. They include honesty, respect, timeliness, communicating clearly, integrity, safety, understanding corporate goals, taking responsibility for your work, teamwork and commitment. This is a thoughtful blog post and I recommend you read it.[19]

---

18 Anna Kelsey-Sugg and Damien Carrick, 18/02/2022, Embellishing the truth in a CV is common. But here's where you can cross the line into fraud https://www.abc.net.au/news/2022-02-18/how-cv-lies-can-become-a-criminal-offence/100809454
19 Belinda Fuller (undated), 12 professional behaviour tips, https://www.katieroberts.com.au/career-advice-blog/12-professional-behaviour-tips/

PART TWO – How to lay the foundation for getting a job

PARALLEL UNIVERSE #2
– AFTER ALEX HAS READ PART ONE AND PART TWO OF
THIS BOOK.

Industry research complete – check! Workplace research complete – check! LinkedIn profile updated – check!

Alas, Alex has not researched the workplace that has advertised the job. Job hunting is frustrating. This must be Alex' one hundredth job application. Thank goodness for résumé templates on the web. Download, fill in, and then just change the job and employer details for each application. Very efficient. You can email off up to five applications every day.

Lou is overworked and understaffed. The right employee would take the pressure off. The responses from last week's ad keep coming in. Over two hundred already. Evaluating them is another job on top of everything else. It wouldn't be so bad if they were all killer candidates, but so far, they all seem hell-bent on sabotaging their chances. None have made the effort to address Lou's carefully crafted job description, so only a few have made it into the *maybe* pile. Returning from a break, Lou sits down to check more emails.

Spam, spam, spam, spam. Oh. Here's one. My new employee perhaps? Bla, bla, bla...promising...résumé attached...hmmm...

I bet they emailed this to 20 employers just today...Lets give them the benefit of doubt...Check them out on LinkedIn. Photo seems friendly...bla, bla, bla... excerpts from college assignments...a bit of work experience...lets look at their résumé...nar...not relevant to me...better suited to a different sector...pity... Lou flicks to the next application...

Imagine working somewhere where you're surrounded by good people, for a supportive boss, in a job that you love and know that you can excel at. That's a recipe for wanting to turn up to work each day! You could be lucky. Some people are. They stumble into a job by accident and end up loving it. That's Daniel Humm's story. He dropped out of school at age 14 and supported himself by working as a kitchen hand. He discovered that he loved cooking. Fast forward 17 years and he runs a three Michelin star restaurant that's also been judged to be the best in the world.[20]

Stories like Daniel's get the microphone because they're uplifting and feel-good. His story is far from the one many people have to tell. Recently I was talking to a fellow I met around a campfire. Just retired, he admitted that in his life he had never managed to find a job he enjoyed. He sounded sad and it made me sad too.

---

luck appears when you're working towards it, not looking for it.

Matashona Dhilwayo said that *luck appears when you're working towards it, not looking for it.*[21] Unlike people who stumble on good luck, I want to show you a way to make your luck. We'll do that by building your *presence* so that it aligns with the job you want. We begin along that path by researching your job before you begin your job search.

As you do your research, prepare to discover that your first career choice may not deliver the level of job satisfaction that you thought it would. If that happens, then perhaps it's time for some soul searching? In his book *What Color Is Your Parachute?* Richard Bolles does a great job of helping you to understand which career you're most likely to excel at.[22] The self-inventory and self-reflection he guides you through is a helpful tool for making an informed career choice. You could easily spend a week completing Richard's,

20 Guy Razz, How I built this podcast, Eleven Madison Park: Daniel Humm, May 5 2021, https://www.npr.org/2021/04/28/991668793/eleven-madison-park-daniel-humm
21 This is such a good saying. Its all over the web. Unfortunately I could not find the original citation for it.
22 What Color Is Your Parachute? 2020: A Practical Manual for Job-Hunters and Career-Changers, Ten Speed Press, 2019.

sometimes confronting tasks. If you're not sure that you've chosen the right career path, then I recommend that you read his book. I promise you that it will be time well spent.[23]

When researching your job, keep in mind my earlier comment that some industry sectors will grow in the aftermath of covid, some will shrink, and where different parts of some businesses are located will change. That understanding speaks to what jobs are likely to continue to be around, what jobs are likely to provide you with career growth opportunities, and how secure your job choice might be.

In the introduction to this book, I talked about the three levels of your *presence pyramid* that form its industry specific base. Now we're going to work on them. The idea behind the pyramid levels is that once you've done a reasonable job of each one, you're ready to graduate to the next. No level is ever complete because as you move up the pyramid, your understanding of the levels below improves.

The foundation of the pyramid (Figure 1) is industry research. That will help you frame your work and education experiences when you create your LinkedIn profile. A good LinkedIn profile will give you greater confidence to network and conduct informational interviews, which in turn, will lead you to do even more research to identify expertise gaps, upgrade your skillset if necessary, and then further refine your LinkedIn profile.

In our quest to build a foundation for understanding your job/industry combination, I'll also talk about internships and the value of volunteer work, and show you how to build an avatar of an employer and their workplace.

Many of you will be familiar with the concept of avatars from your use of web avatars and gravitas, and the 2009 and 2022 Avatar movies. Avatars (also called *personas*) are important tools that we will build in the *industry research* base of your *presence pyramid*. They will give you focus when you create your LinkedIn profile.

---

23 There is a *faith* component to this book that may not be for everyone

---

Your avatars will be fictional characterizations of an employer's key characteristics (age, sex, education, frustrations, motivations, etc). It's an idea that has been around for a long time in marketing circles. Recruiters use them as a tool to help them define the ideal employee for a job.[24] You need to use them as a tool to help you align yourself with your dream job.

I'm about to show you how to create avatars for a typical hiring manager and a typical workplace. These begin as tables that you fill in (e.g. Table 6 and Table 7), and later cut-and-paste to be PowerPoint graphics (e.g. Figure 2 and Figure 3). In part 3 and part 4 I'll show you how to customize these general avatars to a job opportunity (e.g. Table 9 thru Table 14, and Figure 5 thru Figure 10).

Familiarize yourself with the avatar tables and the graphics they become. Some parts are designed to make a hiring manager and their workplace less abstract. Other parts will help you understand expertise gaps that you should close if you want an employer to think of you as a good employee choice.

You can't create an avatar without first doing some research into your dream job. That's what we'll do next.

---

24 For example, Ben Slater, undated, How to Create a Candidate Persona, https://www.beamery.com/resources/blogs/how-to-create-a-candidate-persona

PRESENCE PYRAMID LEVEL 1
– Four ways to research your job

It's not enough to research only a job title. You need to focus on your job in the industry you want to work in. That's because there is a difference between medical equipment sales reps and pharmaceutical sales reps, legal office administrators and medical office administrators, water engineers and road construction engineers, family lawyers and corporate lawyers, hotel baristas and café baristas... If you're struggling to get your head around this idea, then generic job research will suffice to start with. But do be prepared to refine your research as your understanding of your job improves.

If you have an established career, you still need to do this level of research. That's because job titles and job descriptions change over time. If the workplace you're leaving has not kept up with industry trends, you may need to upgrade your training. Imagine looking for a job as an accountant if you'd never used the cloud, as a utility asset manager if you'd never used mapping software, as an ad manager who'd only ever advertised in newspapers, or as a sound engineer who'd only ever used tape recorders.

Employment sites, Google, LinkedIn and YouTube are great resources for job research. For each of the four types of searches I lead you through below, study at least three of your search results and you should start to see trends – important skills, software, OH&S standards, industry buzz words... Write them down. These are things to address in your LinkedIn profile, the avatars you'll create, and in your job applications. Read on to see how easy researching your job can be.

1. Government and recruitment agency websites

Government and recruitment agencies both want you to have a job...

- **Governments:** Because people with jobs pay taxes instead of collecting benefits.
- **Recruiters:** Because when they get someone a job, they earn a placement fee. Some recruiters won't help early career job seekers because the success fee is too small. But, if you make their job easy, some will treat you as a marketing exercise and

still help you. A recruiter told me that he sometimes placed entry level positions for free just to keep himself on his client's radar.

The good news is that both government and recruiters have fantastic online employment research resources these days. They want you to use these so it takes less effort for them to help you one-on-one. Table 3 lists some good starting points. There are lots more.

Table 3: List of government and recruitment career websites.

SITE	COMMENTS
careerplanner.com	Under the Jobs & Job descriptions tab, there's a list of over 12,000 job titles and descriptions.
targetjobs.co.uk/careers-advice/job-descriptions	A–Z of job descriptions that are close to what you might see in an advertised position.
onetonline.org	o-net online not only provides you with job descriptions, it also has functionality for you to search by skill set.
resources.workable.com/job-descriptions	Workable is a recruitment software company. It lists hundreds of job descriptions that employers then customize to their requirements. Other Applicant Tracking System (ATS) businesses have similar resources, but they mostly only make them available to paying customers.
recruitingbrief.com/job-descriptions	As for Workable.com.

2. Google

Google [industry sector] [job] and *"job description"*.
For example...

- "Pharmaceutical sales rep" "job description"
  "Intellectual property lawyer" "job description"
- "Legal office administration" "job description"

- "Health administration" "job description"
- "Barista" "job description"

Also try queries like...

- What's it like to be a [job]
  – What's it like to be a Pharmaceutical sales rep
- What's it like to be a [boss]
  – What's it like to be a Pharmaceutical sales manager
- [job] frustrations
  – Pharmaceutical sales rep frustrations
- [boss] frustrations
  – Pharmaceutical sales manager frustrations

3. YouTube

In the YouTube search box, type the name of a job and industry and "career advice".

For each of the examples below, there were at least ten results worth looking at, sometimes hundreds. Here's five examples...

- *Intellectual property lawyer career advice*
- *Legal office administration career advice*
- *Health administration career advice*
- *Barista career advice*
- *Pharmaceutical sales rep career advice*
  I drilled further into the *pharmaceutical sales* query to show you the sort of information you can find out. Here's the first five results...

  – How to get into pharmaceutical sales without experience

  – How to get into Pharmaceutical Sales

  – The Reality Of Pharmaceutical Medical Sales Jobs

  – Life as a Medical Representative | Pharmaceutical Sales

  – My Pharmaceutical Sales Rep Job Nightmare

After watching three YouTube videos about being a pharmaceutical sales rep, I discovered five things that would not have found out by just by looking at written job descriptions...

1. There are many paths to becoming a pharmaceutical sales rep.
2. A degree with a technical orientation is preferred.
3. You can do online courses to get a basic pharma sales rep certification.
4. The job can involve lots of sitting in medical waiting rooms,
5. You spend lots of time organizing seminars and lunches with doctors.

4. LinkedIn

On LinkedIn, find people who are currently working in the job you want to do (preferably 2–5 years ahead of you). In the search box, type terms like *intern [job]*. That will return people who are currently an intern or were previously an intern.

For the people you find, where did they work and what did they do there? Maybe they're workplaces that employ interns? If you look at enough people, you should start to see a pattern of career progress... how long they stay in their job roles for, whether they change companies to progress their career, etc.

Now take the time to compare yourself with people doing jobs that are at, or are one promotion along from the level you'll be starting at. How do you stack up against them? Start to think about the mini research projects and additional short courses you might need to do to align yourself with the skillsets of someone who's already settled into that position.

You need to research the industry your job is within as well

The final piece of your job research puzzle is to research the industry you want to work in. That will give you context for your job. In the course of your job research, you should have come across the names of businesses that might employ you. Google *[business name] "annual report"* to find an annual report for a business. If the business does not issue public reports, then find a similar business that does. In many places, businesses listed on the stock exchange, not for profits, and some government businesses, are obliged by law to make their annual reports public. I'll talk more about using company reports for job intelligence later in this section, and also in part four of this book.

Skim the annual report to get a feel for how the business is performing, and why its performing in the way it is. These days, many annual reports make use of infographics and summary dot points to make them easy to understand. Here's an example of what I mean. Recently I bought some outdoor gear. Out of interest, I googled the Macpac outdoor equipment retailer (I typed *macpac annual report). I learnt that...*

- It's one of 4 retailers in the Super Retail group of companies.
  - This means that there may be opportunities in the Super Retail group of companies as well as in the Macpac retail business.
- It's growing both instore and online.
  - You would need to delve deeper to understand if the business will slow down when covid slows, or if it will survive its competition and become the dominant player.
- It has environmental and social standards.
  - This means that there may be opportunities for people with environmental degrees as well as the more obvious business and retail oriented qualifications.
- The annual report sums up the opportunities for business, marketing, retail, logistics and computing job seekers in a slide called "key opportunities to create shareholder value".
  - The Super Retail group has a focus on loyalty schemes, digital engagement, logistics, smart buying, formal training for retail staff, tailoring offers to customers and stores, store performance analyses, and more.

The trick for you is to set yourself ahead of your job seeking competition. Use the information you find in annual reports to align yourself with a business' ambitions, and if necessary, the ambitions of its parent group too. Often these ambitions are clearly articulated in annual reports. So, for each annual report you read, ask yourself what you could do to help that business achieve

---

its goals? Are there gaps in your training that you need to fill to address these?

Do work experience that's relevant to the job you want

Based on your industry research, you should have an understanding of what the workplace expectations are for your job. Now you need relevant work experience. In the absence of that, having worked anywhere is better than having worked nowhere. Work experience is important for two reasons...

1. Any job you've had demonstrates to an employer that someone once had the confidence to hire you and that you had the discipline to be a reliable employee. It's what marketers call *social* proof. Which widget would you buy – the one with, or the one without online reviews? Even jobs like babysitting, trolley collecting, and sports umpiring are better than nothing.

2. Relevant work experience is best. It demonstrates that you have the potential to be useful from day one.

The more you put yourself out there, the more things you can add to your portfolio, and the more likely you are to stumble on opportunity. For example, as a teenager I won an apprenticeship in the furniture trades through a part time job polishing silver in an antique shop. Another time I won a full time research job after doing holiday work for one of my professors. As a consultant, I often won work by reputation rather than by responding to advertisements. Ask older friends and family. You'll be surprised at the number of stories like that.

Internships and volunteering are a great way to get relevant work experience. They are also a good way to make yourself known (and impress) people who might hire you.

Internships

It's common for colleges and universities to form partnerships with corporations that include internship opportunities, usually for an agreed number of students. Other times, internships are advertised by businesses directly. Some are during term break. Others are part time during the year. Internships are often formal arrangements

Internships can also be informal arrangements. Recently I was speaking to a senior staff member at a global financial organization. He said that his work often had interns – usually a staff member's child, neighbor, or some similar connection. Their model is to let an intern sit with different staff members for a day or two each, over a two or three week period.

Start by googling *[your city] internship.* Be aware that the higher up an internship appears in the search results the more competitive it will be. You'll have a better chance of finding an internship if you use your network.

Put yourself in an employer's boots. Why would they offer internships and work experience programs in the first place? A common reason is that it's a low cost way to scout for staff who will fit into their workplace. Some businesses are coy about the possibilities, and others are upfront about them. One ad I saw had this dot point *fast track yourself into the [company name] Management Trainee (Graduate) program 2024.*

It's common for interns to think that they'll use their college training from day one. Sorry to be the bearer of bad news. You're thinking about this issue only from your viewpoint and not the employer's. It rarely happens that way. You need to prove you can do the basics first, so expect to do menial tasks to start with.

You cannot expect a business to risk its reputation by throwing an unknown and inexperienced worker at a project from day one. Expect research internships to involve lots of data formatting rather than report writing, and law internships to involve research more than client contact.

Aside from the obvious (doing tasks that are unlawful or unsafe, or *mostly* tasks that you weren't hired to do), "*that's not my job*" should not be in your vocabulary. Especially in a small workplace, someone has to check the photocopier or tidy the tea room. If it's not you on a small hourly rate (or free), it may be the CEO who's billable at hundreds of dollars an hour. That's not to say that you should automatically do all the rotten jobs. But, you should at least do your share.

In many jurisdictions there are laws against taking advantage of interns, and rules for determining what should be paid work and what should be unpaid training. You should seek advice from your educational institution if you're unsure whether you're being treated correctly.

That said, trainees cost an organization money because they take resources away from productive work. You need to show some level of appreciation for that. Its not a time to be anything other than happy that you're in the same space as people who have the ability to hire you.

Volunteering

If you can't secure an internship, you should consider volunteering.

Volunteering is a good way to gain relevant work experience, and to demonstrate your core values to a potential employer. Environmental, refugee, homeless, aged care and other types of volunteering each demonstrate different core values.

Most charities and not for profits have volunteer programs. This sector needs all the same skillsets that the business sector needs. Although they often can't afford to pay you, they can provide you with experience and training (and often a reference as well). Some of the bigger charities even have formalized training paths for volunteers.

Google *volunteer [where you live]* and you should see dozens of opportunities (e.g. *volunteer London, volunteer New York City, volunteer Melbourne*).

When I googled *volunteer Melbourne* and *volunteer trainee*, I was presented with gardening, environmental, disability, aged care, administration, marketing, IT and retail opportunities. One organization even offered a $2500 training qualification in return for a volunteering commitment.

You can also find volunteer opportunities by just knocking on doors – community houses, community radio stations and charity shops are just three examples.

Do not underestimate the value that volunteering can have for your career. Aside from the possibility of discovering that you enjoy the not for profit sector, senior volunteers have been known to scout for talent to employ in their own private businesses. Think about it. Volunteer gardening projects will be run by professional gardeners, cooking projects by professional chefs, offices by experienced administrators, community legal services by established lawyers, etc. Even if the coordinators are retired, they're still likely to have contacts in the industry.

Before you commit to a volunteer position, be sure that you're going to get the level of training that you're hoping for. Like any sector, expect there to be good employers and bad employers. You should google terms like *what's it like to work for [organization name]*. Expect sites like glassdoor, indeed, quora and reddit to return results, especially for larger organizations.

You may have problems finding reviews for smaller volunteer organizations. You'll have to ask around to find out about them. Expect some to be too closely tied to niche careers for anyone to be brave enough to write a negative review. Imagine how hard it would be to get a job as a paleontologist if you publicly criticized your time as a volunteer at your national dinosaur museum.

Keep in mind that reviews are left by the sorts of people who leave reviews. Some people are never satisfied, and others are easily satisfied. If a review doesn't sound right, google the reviewer's name to find other reviews by them. If their pattern is to generally leave positive reviews, then their negative review is worth noting. But if they usually leave negative reviews, then maybe they're just someone who likes to complain.

Sometimes you'll need to just seize a volunteering opportunity and see how it works out for you. If it doesn't work out, be sure to leave on good terms. That way, at least if an employer calls them for a reference they'll be able to say things like you were "friendly, hardworking and punctual". Which of course, you were!

If you become aware that there's expertise gaps between your volunteer training, and the training you identified in your industry research, you should fill these gaps with training from sites like YouTube, Khan Academy, Udemy, Coursera, Udacity, LinkedIn Learning, Masterclass, Codecademy, Alison, edx, etc.

Avatars: A tool to understand an employer's problems, hopes and dreams[25]

All along, I've been borrowing ideas from marketers to bolster your *presence* and make you saleable to an employer. In contrast to mass marketing campaigns for lots of sales of low value products like sweets and soft drinks, your highly focused micro-campaign will aim to attract a handful of high-value customers, one of whom will employ you.

Any marketer will tell you that its no sense selling a product that nobody wants to buy. Sometimes it's not your product that stinks,

---

You don't just accept who you find – you choose who you attract.

---

but rather who you're trying to sell it to, or how you're pitching it. For example, you'll find it hard to get a job as a business analyst or an engineer if your *presence* only speaks to your sports or theatre achievements. Even if you know that you're the perfect fit for a workplace, it's not an employer's job to draw the links between your poorly articulated skillset and their needs. They don't have the time or the energy to do that. Hence Brian Clark's comment that *you don't just accept who you find – you choose who you attract.*[26]

---

25 **Resources**
Google image search – "job seeker persona"
Katrina Benco, 5 Signs You're Creating Personas That Won't Be Effective, https://bit.ly/Katrina-Benco
Loz James, How To Create a Customer Avatar In 5 Simple Steps, March 28, 2018 https://www.contentchampion.com/customer-avatar
Website that guides you through the basics of creating an avatar https://hubspot.com/make-my-persona

---

The key to your successful micro-campaign is to align your skills and values with an employer's needs. So, when you know who you want to attract, next you need to articulate what their needs are. Their needs are not always obvious. The creation of an *avatar*[27], a fictional characterization of an employer's key attributes like their age, sex, motivations, frustrations, education, etc. is key to that.

So, let's get a bit concrete with what I mean. By going through the process of creating an avatar, you will discover which new skills you need to learn if you are to be a dream-hire. Whether you need to do additional training to bolster any weak areas. Whether your hiring manager has any pain points that you could help with.

Imagine a hiring manager's delight in reading an application from someone who has the right skillset, outlook, work ethic, degree, references, work experience, and also understands their business.

Your synthesized understanding of a workplace as articulated in the avatars you create will help you be that person. It's another ingredient to the recipe that will make employers notice you, and make the decision to hire you an easy one.

The problems, hopes and dreams that you articulate in your avatars are also going to inform the way you approach your LinkedIn profile.

I'm the first to admit that *avatars* seem a bit "markety" and abstract if you've not come across them before. I want you to stay with me on this because avatars are a key tool that will help you put yourself into your hiring manager's boots. Empathy is an important ingredient in a good job application.

Some bits of your avatars may seem a bit creepy at first. But that's a necessary evil. They're for your personal use so you can anonymize the creepy bits when you've finished, or even delete them. Even if they're a new idea to you, they're a standard tool in many recruiters' tool kits![28]

26 Clark, Brian, 2017, *How to Attract Your Ideal Customer with Perfectly Positioned Content,* https://www.copyblogger.com/who
27 Also called a persona
28 For example, Ben Slater, undated, How to Create a Candidate Persona, https://www.beamery.com/resources/blogs/how-to-create-a-candidate-persona

Avatars are important because the greater the depth of your understanding of your employer, the more easily you'll be able find them, and the more effectively you'll be able to communicate with them. The more specific you can be the better.

We'll create your avatars as PowerPoint graphics. You can download the examples from the downloads area below the accompanying video.[29] Creating them will force you to synthesize your industry research into succinct dot points. They will help you...

1. Craft a story about yourself that has your employer's problems, hopes and dreams front and center.

2. Home in on employers who are more likely to be receptive to what you have to offer.

Your avatars will serve as a reference point for anything you write or communicate about yourself. Armed with the insights that you synthesize, these tools will help you frame your skills and values in a way that align and resonate with an employer. That will give you a better chance of being seen as the solution to their problems, rather than an annoying and unfocussed job applicant.

Of the 10 information areas that I describe below, the frustrations area is by far the most important. Let's look at some examples of frustrations that you might identify for your hiring manager's avatar, and how you'd deal with them in a job application...

-   Sample frustration: Scheduling shift workers is time consuming and messy.
    -   Response in your application: Maybe you know a way to make the scheduling job less painful? Use examples from previous jobs to demonstrate that you're reliable.
-   Sample frustration: There's lots of data but nobody is turning it into useful information.
    -   Response in your application: Brush up on some tools and techniques to deal with the type of data they're having problems with. Find out which software is commonly used

---

29 https://bit.ly/wsjsd-2-3

by that industry and build your skills in it. Then you can present yourself as someone who is able to turn their type of data into useful information.

- Sample frustration: Narrow skillsets of staff is hampering good communication between business sections.
    - Response in your application: Demonstrate that you have a broad skillset that's relevant to multiple areas in the workplace. Then focus on one or two of your skills that are relevant to the job you're applying for. You can achieve breadth of expertise by watching YouTube videos and enrolling in inexpensive courses on sites like Udemy.

You reinforce your new found expertise in your LinkedIn profile by linking to interesting blog posts about your hiring manager's frustrations. Ideally, you would write a blog post about them.

You need to create two avatars...

1. Your hiring manager: That's the person who will report to in your new job.
2. Your workplace: That's the business that you want a job in. This avatar provides context for your job within the business.

Let's start with your hiring manager. An overview of the ten information areas for their avatar is shown in Table 4, and in detail in Table 6. Sorry, but level of detail in Table 6 can't be helped if I am to give you a feel for the range of things that you might want to add to your avatar graphic. Take a moment to study it, and get your head around how that might translate into the graphic in Figure 2.[30] You might also want to look at the three worked examples of hiring manager avatars in part four.

---

30 Download from https://bit.ly/wsjsd-2-3

Table 4: The ten information areas for a hiring manager's avatar

ITEM	DESCRIPTION
Overview	Download a stock photo from the web of someone who you think your hiring manager might look like. Then summarize things like their age, education and personality traits.
	Use one of the personality traits listed in Table 5. Many of these personality traits are unattractive. That's because there are bad bosses out there. Forums like reddit are full of bad boss stories. Forewarned is forearmed!
Performance measures	How is their performance measured? Increased sales, increased profit, trouble free computer systems, manufacturing up-time, ...?
Bio	A paragraph about them. That part of their history that's relevant to their job. And their aspirations in their role.
Quote	A short quote that summarizes their key characteristics.
Motivations	What motivates them? Profit? Ideology? Sense of achievement?
Role and responsibilities	What are their responsibilities. How involved are they in each? Do they manage staff?
Goals	Do they want to create more products, more efficient systems, a better customer experience, something else?
Frustrations	What drives them nuts? Staffing issues, data management, inefficient systems, old systems, ...?
Influences	Who and what influences them?
Software/apps	What software do they use. Are they satisfied with them? Are they skilled at using them?

*Table 5: Labels to insert in the personality trait section of your avatar.
Many of these traits are unattractive. I've included them to make you aware
that there are unattractive people like that out there![31]*

LABEL TO USE IN THE AVATAR OVERVIEW AREA.	DESCRIPTION
Milker	Thinks of employees as milking machine and is only concerned with how to make money from you.
Sexist	The gender biased boss prefers to have either female or male employees.
Power hungry military	Expects full compliance and focused on results. Yells and threaten employees to get results.
Micromanager	The perfectionist. Finds fault in everything that you do and practices over involvement in your job.
Old school	Has a fixed mindset and dwells on the way things used to be inside the workplace. They are resistant to new ways of doing things.
Prime mover	The brain behind the innovation.
Advocate	Aims for ways to promote eco-friendliness. Philanthropic.
Affiliative	Thinks that employees are assets and places importance on creating connections to them and having harmony in the workplace.
Best bud	Wants to be treated as equal and is very friendly to employees.
Lone wolf	Doesn't want to socialize beyond office time and premises.

It's possible that avatars already exist for your hiring manager and new workplace. Search for them on Google using terms like [job/employer] persona/avatar (e.g. *"tax accountant" avatar, "tax accountant" persona*). Be sure to use quotes so that Google does an exact match.

Use what you find as inspiration for the avatars that you're creating. They may have been created for a different purpose than yours, so do not use them without incorporating your own research and making them your own.

31   Table provided by Ginabelle Dasalla, September 2020

*Table 6: Hiring manager avatar. See numbers in Figure 2. ***

HEADING	YOUR BOSS – SUGGESTIONS FOR ANSWERS
OVERVIEW (1)	
Photo: You need to be able to visualize your avatar. Find a photo of someone who looks like the sort of person you'd like to work for.	Preferably a stock photo (e.g. pxhere.com, freeimages.com, commons.wikimedia.org). Only use famous people if that's who you're aspiring to work for.
Name:	Use an imaginary name.
Age	Use an age range (e.g. 25–35).
Job title	Manager of ?
Personality traits	Dominantly [gender]. Or the gender you'd prefer to work for. Dominantly [personality trait from Table 5].
Income	Use an actual figure if you know it, or your industry research if you don't.
Reports to	Position name.
Education	List of qualifications: Diploma/degree/other qualification in [skill] from [institution].
Count of staff	Team of ? people.
PERFORMANCE MEASURES (2)	
Performance measures	Some/all of business' performance measures will apply to your hiring manager (e.g. # satisfied clients, # improved services, # improved processes, good workplace morale, etc.)
BIO (3)	
Bio	Tell a story about your avatar in ~100 words. LinkedIn profiles can help seed ideas.
QUOTE (4)	
Quote	Find a quote that sums up a key characteristic or problem they have.
MOTIVATIONS (5)	
Money	**Profit:** Sell more, make more,...
Values: What is important to them? What drives the decisions they make?	**Teamwork:** Build a happy and cohesive team. **Ideology:** Ensure purchases under their control adhere to company standards. **Promotion:** Climbing the corporate ladder. Higher wages/more responsibility/more staff **Quality:** Focus on production quality.

HEADING	YOUR BOSS – SUGGESTIONS FOR ANSWERS
ROLE AND RESPONSIBILITY (6)	
Overseeing implementations (25%)	Ensuring systems are implemented with minimal interruptions.
Writing specifications (30%)	Specifying new system features.
Designing features (20%)	Designing how the features look.
Meetings (15%)	Meetings to discuss all aspects of the business. Including board meetings.
User testing (10%)	Testing features prior to implementation.
GOALS (7)	
Expand business	Improve the customer experience (e.g. via ordering app). Open new shop/office, offer more products.
Staff supervision	Step back from day-to-day micro-management issues. Less staff supervision & increased focus on strategy.
Streamline business	Streamline production. Tame business data.
FRUSTRATIONS (8)	
Hard to find qualified staff	Recruiting is time consuming and EXTRA work.
Staff availability is unreliable	Too much time wasted reorganizing shifts.
Teamwork	Lack of alignment when working with multiple teams.
Systems: Current processes complicated and stressful. There must be a better way.	Too much time spent on micro-managing projects.
Systems: Data overload	Masses of data, but no tools to easily manage and summarize it.
Systems: Lack of expertise	Already overworked. No time to learn and implement new systems.
Constraints	Limited IT support. Narrow skillset of staff.
INFLUENCES (9)	
Influences	Competitors, colleagues, blogs, entrepreneur influencers.
SOFTWARE (10)	
Office suite, CRM, ...	Office suite (MS, OpenOffice, ...) Accounting suit (Xero/reckon/MYOB) Customer Relationship Management (CRM) software.

Download this table from https://bit.ly/wsjsd-2-3. The items in the cells are examples of the types of things you could put into your graphic, and are there for illustration only.

Table 7: Workplace avatar: See numbers in Figure 3

HEADING	THE BUSINESS – SUGGESTIONS FOR ANSWERS
OVERVIEW (1)	
Photo: You need to be able to visualize your avatar. Find a photo that represents a widget they sell, or service they provide.	Preferably a stock photo (e.g. pxhere.com, freeimages.com, commons.wikimedia.org). Only use famous products or services if that's who you're aspiring to work for.
Name of business	Use an imaginary name. (e.g. Widgets Inc.)
Time in business	Use a range (e.g. 5–10 years)
Employees	Number of employees.
Income	An indication of the size of the business. Google [business name] "annual income" for a business that's representative of the type of workplace that appeals to you.
PERFORMANCE MEASURES (2)	
Performance measures	· Satisfied investors · Annual growth >15% · Raving customers
BIO (3)	
Bio	Tell a short story about your avatar. What exactly does the business do? Where does it operate? How many staff does it have?
QUOTE (4)	
Quote	Find a quote that sums up a key characteristic of the business. E.g. "We want our widgets to be renowned for their quality and our business for its customer service".
MOTIVATIONS (5)	
Money	**Profit:** Sell more, make more,...
Values: What is important to them? What drives the decisions they make?	**Ideology:** Ensure adherence to company standards **Teamwork:** Build a happy and cohesive team. **Quality:** Focus on production quality
Clients (6)	
Clients	What does a typical client look like? a. Business-to-Business (B2B)? b. Business-to-customer (B2C)? c. Other departments in the business? d. All of the above? Why do clients do business with them and not some other business? Are client's "niche" in some way?

HEADING	THE BUSINESS – SUGGESTIONS FOR ANSWERS
Client pain points and frustrations	Is there a common theme to customer complaints? *What could you do to prevent such complaints?* a. Don't take credit card. b. Delay b/w order & delivery too great. c. Invoices incompatible with cloud accounting systems. d. Poor product documentation.
Geography	Eastern metro.
GOALS (7)	
Systems	New production line systems. New project management systems. New office systems. New customer engagement systems.
FRUSTRATIONS (8)	
Hard to find qualified staff	Recruiting is time consuming and EXTRA work.
Staff availability is unreliable	Too much time wasted reorganizing shifts.
Systems: Office	Zero skill overlap means teams are not aligned.
Systems: Current processes complicated and stressful.	Too much time spent on managing projects.
Systems: Data overload	Masses of data, but no tools to easily manage and summarize it.
Systems: Lack of expertise	We're rolling out new systems & software, but nobody knows how to use them.
Productivity	Lots of work being done, but too little of it is productive.
Constraints	Limited IT support. Narrow skillset of staff.
EMPLOYEE BENEFITS (9)	
Benefit	Annual leave, sick leave, childcare, pension, flexible hours, work at home or office, health insurance.
SOFTWARE (10)	
Office suite, CRM, ...	a. Office suite (MS, OpenOffice, ...). b. Accounting suit (Xero / reckon / MYOB). c. Customer Relationship Management (CRM) software.

* Download this table from https://bit.ly/wsjsd-2-3

Figure 2: The hiring manager avatar graphic. See numbers in Table 6*

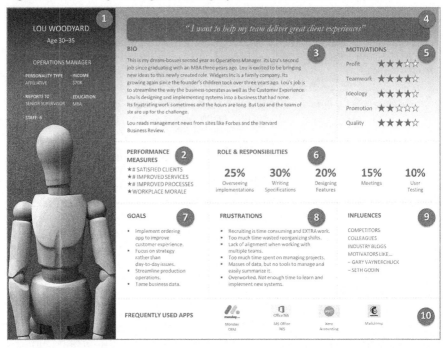

Figure 3: The workplace avatar graphic. See numbers in Table 7*

* *Download these figures from the downloads area at https://bit.ly/wsjsd-2-3*
Download this from the web link at the QR code.

Now compare Table 6 to Figure 2 and Table 7 to Figure 3. Note how the rows in the table become items in the graphic. This is a good time to watch the video that accompanies this section.

Now that I've walked you through an example, create an avatar for your ideal workplace. As was the case for your employer's' avatar, there's 10 information areas to fill in. I show you the headings and give examples of possible answers in Table 7 and a worked example in Figure 3.

After you've created your avatars, lay them out in front of you and study them.

PRESENCE PYRAMID LEVEL 2: Craft your LinkedIn profile to target a job

It's easy to be intimidated by LinkedIn. Don't be. Yes, there are some things that will work better if you get them 100% right. That's the case with most things you do on the web. Don't over think it. If you can send a text message or post to social media, then you can fill in a LinkedIn profile. That's right. *Fill in* – mostly small chunks of information about yourself.

When you're being chased by a lion, you only need to be faster than the person running next to you!

You're not Oprah Winfrey or Richard Branson. You just need some web real estate to showcase your professionalism. Nobody expects you to have the profile that a seasoned professional would. Just one that's appropriate for someone who's starting out. When you're being chased by a lion, you only need to be faster than the person running next to you! In other words, your profile only needs to be better than the other job candidates you're competing with. The good news is that your LinkedIn profile is not set in stone. Don't get overcome with analysis paralysis. Just get something down and change it as your understanding of your new job improves.

A good LinkedIn profile is far more than just your work and study history. It is somewhere employers can go to discreetly find out more about you in their own time, and so reduce the friction of getting to know you. It's your chance to showcase the type of work that interests you and the quality of work that you're capable of producing. That you can write a succinct summary of your work. That you're able to draw links between your experiences and what your industry wants.

A crafted LinkedIn profile is a chance to demonstrate your professionalism. It should send an *explicit* message to your new employer that you're a good communicator and would make a valuable employee. It should also send an *implicit* message that because you'd make a valuable employee, there's a chance that they may need to compete for you (ie. you're preparing them to employ you at the upper end of the position's wage range).

Creating your LinkedIn profile is an important steppingstone for writing your résumé. It is an opportunity for self-reflection, so it's important to approach the process with an open mind. It's a place to address the hiring manager and workplace's problems, hopes and dreams that you articulated in their avatars. Just going through the process of creating your profile will give you new insights into your new job, force you to write about your capabilities in a way that's relevant to an employer, and give you greater confidence to perform the best you can in networking situations.

Think of LinkedIn as a three-legged stool. Take one leg away and the stool will fall over. Let's have a look at the three legs...

First: A completed profile: You should aim for a completed profile that's crafted to target your hiring manager and workplace avatars, and optimized be easily harvested by LinkedIn and other web robots. Done properly, a hiring manager will have a better chance of finding you, and, once they've found you, hopefully your profile will be interesting enough to encourage them to take the time to find out that you're not only relevant to their workplace, but also that you'd make a great addition to it.

Second: A maintained LinkedIn profile: You need to maintain your LinkedIn profile. While you're in job search mode, make a habit of regularly reviewing your profile to reflect your improved understanding of your industry and the workplaces that you might be targeting.

Third: Network and relationship building: The more you participate on LinkedIn the more its algorithm will learn about you. That leads to more relevant connection suggestions for you, and a greater chance that you will show up as a relevant connection suggestion to other people (including hiring managers).

Find LinkedIn profiles to use as inspiration

In the LinkedIn search bar, search for [your job] intern (e.g. *"civil engineer" intern)* and choose the *in people* category from the suggestions that appear. Many of the results will have a subtitle that reads *current: [job] intern (e.g. current: civil engineer intern)* or *past: [job] intern (e.g. past: civil engineer intern).*

Look at the LinkedIn profiles of people who are currently doing the job you want, and people up to a couple of years ahead of you in their career. Pick people whose profile is complete, who are active and have more than just a few connections. Ignore profiles with headlines like "student at University", "founder" or similar. Such headlines suggest that the person is unlikely to be LinkedIn savvy.

Read as many of these profiles as you can. You need to get a feel for how LinkedIn savvy early career people in your industry go about filling in their profiles. What types of things do they write about? What's their writing "voice" like – are they academic or conversational? Don't be concerned if you can't find good examples. That may indicate that there's an opportunity for you to stand out from the crowd. Try searching profiles for a related job instead.

There's a great podcast episode about LinkedIn profiles on Jeffery Shaw's *Self employed life.* Jeffery interviews a LinkedIn specialist called Marissa Polselli.[32] Marissa talks a lot about putting your

---

32 Jeffrey Shaw, The Self Employed Life podcast, Episode 647, Marissa Polselli – LinkedIn for Personal Brands, https://www.jeffreyshaw.com/post/marissa-polselli-linkedin-for-personal-brands

heart into your LinkedIn profile. She has some really good advice. You should check Jeffery Shaw's and Marissa Polselli's LinkedIn profiles out. They're gold standard. Professional but not salesy.

What not to do on LinkedIn

It's obvious to me, but I think that I it still need to say it... **LinkedIn is not social media!** LinkedIn is a place to showcase your professionalism. Everything you add to your profile must relate back to the avatars you created.

- **If your profile is full of spelling mistakes:** That makes you look careless.

- **If your profile only contains basic information:** An employer may wonder if you really want a job, or if you'd be capable of building and maintaining professional relationships in a post covid online work environment.

- **Sexualised photos of yourself are unprofessional:** They send a message that you'll treat your workplace like a night club.

- **Swearing and street language are unprofessional:** Unless you're in an industry that uses street language, greetings like "*Yo Bro*" sends the message that you don't understand that there's a time and place to be professional.

- **Joke posts are unprofessional:** They send a message that you'll spend all day on social media rather than doing what you're paid to do.

- **A quirky vanity url is unprofessional:** Unless you want to be a comedy writer, it sends a message that you can't take things seriously.

- **Social media posts showing the space cadet or drunken you are unprofessional:** Some employers will look at your social media profiles as well as your LinkedIn profile. Posts like these send a message that you'll be hungover on Mondays and that you'll behave inappropriately at work functions.

Faced with hundreds of applicants for an advertised job, an employer's first task is to eliminate candidates. Few employers will be willing to align themselves with anyone who strays far from middle of the road behavior.

How to fill in your LinkedIn profile

Figure 4: Annotated screen capture of my LinkedIn profile. The numbers relate the headings below.

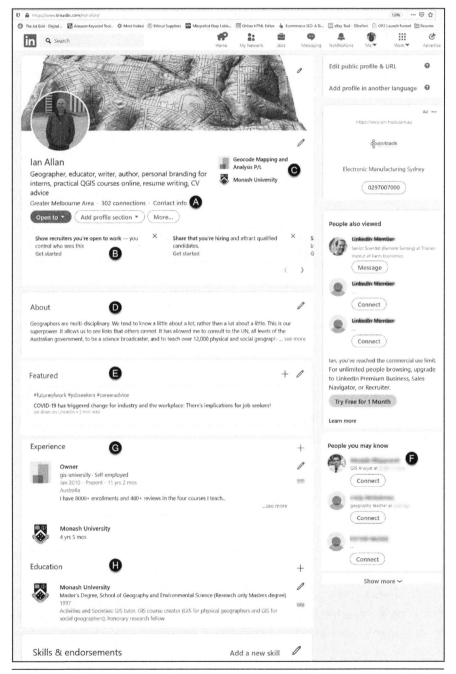

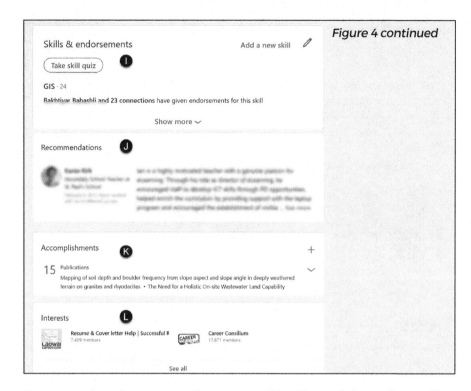

Figure 4 continued

I'm assuming that most of you have filled in social media profiles before, so I'm only going to give you general instructions for how to fill in your LinkedIn profile. Besides, dialogs in social media change frequently, so anything I write would soon be out of date.

You view and edit your profile from within the "Me" dropdown menu in the top right corner. Click that and you'll be presented with a dialog box like the one in Figure 4. Your LinkedIn profile is compartmentalized into sections. Most sections are easy to fill in. Some items can be edited in more than one place. As you will see, there are some tricks with some sections. The following headings refer the A–L labels in Figure 4.

Contact information (A)

This is where you provide your contact information. Fill in as much as you can. Test any links you insert to make sure they work. If you have a smarty-pants email or social media address, get a new one! Having a silly name is self sabotage. It makes you look unprofessional.

- **Your profile:** Change the default LinkedIn address to be your first and last name. If that's not available, then adding your profession as a suffix to your name is one approach to making your name unique in a meaningful way. For example, *ian-allan-geographer* looks more professional than *ian-allan-86*.
- **Website:** Add your website address if you have one. Your site should look professional and be relevant to the job you want. By that I mean that if you have a book review website, its unlikely to be relevant to an employer unless you're reviewing books that are relevant to your industry, or the employer is connected to the publishing industry. Or, if you have an esports website, that's probably only relevant to a gaming tech business. Creatives may choose to insert a link to their portfolio on a site like Pinterest. Be sure to remove any inappropriate and nonprofessional pins first.
- **Email:** Your best email address. One that you monitor. Not a smarty-pants address.
- **Twitter:** Enter your twitter address if you tweet about your profession, and in a professional manner.

Job preferences (B)

It's important to tell people that you're looking for work. This is where you say that, the type of work you're looking for, where you'd like to work (geographically), and when you're available to start. There are options you can check to say that you're looking for full time, part time, contract or temporary work, and even an internship.

Intro section (C)

This is another place where you add information about yourself. Things like your name, location, industry, and education. Everything here is obvious, except the headline area which is VERY important.

Headline

You need enough industry relevant keywords in your headline so that the people you want to find you, can. Think about why someone might be searching for someone with your skillset, and what you can do to make it easy for them to find you.

Let's be honest about this. A software engineer is unlikely to be found if their headline describes them as *student at university*, or *founder and CEO* of some enterprise they've started. Who searches for a "founder"? Who searches for a "student"? Something like *[your job] seeking internship*, or *[your job] seeking entry level position* is far more likely to get you found.

Search engines continue to get smarter. These days they prepopulate searches based on popular search terms. You can use these prepopulated search words as *keywords*. In the LinkedIn search bar, type a term that you think describes you (e.g software engineer). If no search suggestions appear, then LinkedIn is telling you that people don't search using that term, so try a different one. Also, if your research shows that you qualify for some government training incentive, then you should add that to your headline.

- **Bad headline:**
  - *Student at university*
  - *Founder of ABC co.*

- **Good headline:**
  - *Software engineer*
  - *Civil engineer seeking internship – Social media marketer (qualifies for [some govt trainee incentive])*
  - *Hospitality marketer seeking graduate position (qualifies for $10,000 government trainee incentive).*

Photos

Photos are important because they're a visual key that makes it easier for someone to remember you, and maybe even seek you out at an event. They're also an opportunity to send a subtle message to an employer that you would fit in to their workplace.

You can add two bitmaps (png or jpg), and reposition, zoom in or out, or rotate them if you need to.

Inset photo (headshot): Dimensions are 400–7680 pixels wide by 400–4320 pixels high.

Use a friendly looking photo of yourself that fits in with the hiring manager avatar that you created. If your avatar wears a light blue open necked business shirt, then that (or something similar) is what you should wear in your photo.

If you only like working in loud t-shirts, then sure, wear a loud t-shirt in your photo. But do that with the knowledge that those workplaces where blue open-necked business shirts are the de facto uniform, may be less likely to reach out to you.

It's important to work somewhere you feel comfortable being yourself. Maybe things like dress expectations are a clue that you need to go back to the job research drawing board to find a more compatible sector within your chosen industry. An example that comes to mind is the different dress expectations of Fortune 500 companies compared to the dress expectations of the creative sector.

Your photo will be cropped to be round. Choose to add an eye catching surround with #OPENTOWORK written on it. That will make you stand out in the *people you may know* and *people also viewed* sections. It also tells the LinkedIn algorithm to show your profile to hiring managers.

Background photo: LinkedIn recommends 1584 (w) x 396 (h) pixels. Up to 8MB.

Preferably a photo/bitmap that draws a link between you and your industry. For example, a cartographer might use a photo of a drone, or a bitmap of a thematic map they created.

This is a nice-to-have, but is not essential. Google's *image search* is a great resource for these. There's lots of image search options, including an ability to choose an image by its color and usage rights. Click the *tools* button in Google's *image search* to access these features.

- **Image color:** If you're wearing a light blue shirt in your photo then you could request that Google only shows you images that are dominantly blue.
- **Image usage rights:** Don't breach copyright. Click the usage *rights button* and choose to display only imagery that have

CREATIVE COMMONS LICENSES. Also check royalty free image sites like pxhere.com, freeimages.com and commons. wikimedia.org.

Location and industry

Fill in your country of residence, the region within that country, and your industry. This helps LinkedIn make geographically and industry relevant suggestions to link you with other people, and other people with you.

About (D)

Your *about* section should talk to your target audience's wants, needs and fears. Be brave when describing yourself.

After having researched your industry (ie. the base of your *presence pyramid*), and created avatars for an employer and a workplace, you should have an idea about some of the things you need to put into here.

The easiest way to approach this is to refer to the LinkedIn profiles you used for inspiration. Study their *about* sections.

You want people to be able to easily find you, so be sure to use *keywords.* I discussed this idea when I talked about filling in your *industry headline (3).* Use the LinkedIn search bar to help you. If the word you type doesn't appear, then try related words until you find one that does. As an example, the keyword *email lists* returns only company results (bad), but *email marketing* returns results in LinkedIn's jobs, services, people and groups categories (good).

Featured content (E)

The featured content area is a great place to show your wares.

This area is important because it builds your credibility in the eyes of anyone who looks at your profile. It tells them that you're someone who participates in your profession and doesn't just spectate. It's a low-key way for them to get a feel for what makes you tick. And, if you regularly add content that's aligned with the avatars you created, it's also making you look like you might be a useful person to have around.

Lots of people suffer from imposter syndrome when it comes to posting on social media. Don't talk yourself down. Your opinions are important too, even if you're a newcomer to your industry.

Anyhow, it's not like the whole world is going to be reading your posts. The reality is that only a few people will ever see them. Those that do will probably just be impressed that a graduate is participating in their industry. Think about it. Do you critically examine every LinkedIn post you see? Probably not. So why would you think that a bunch of other people would be bothered to take the time to judge your posts either?

The more you put your thoughts and ideas out there, the easier and more natural having an opinion and writing about it will become. I have my own story that illustrates that point.

Years ago, I was invited to sit in on a radio show. Half an hour in, the host looked across the panel and announced that she'd *defer to her studio guest for an opinion on that*. I sat there like a store dummy. Nothing came out. I didn't think I had anything important to say. It was terrible radio. Most radio announcers have a similar tale to tell. Fortunately, a friend encouraged me to come back another time. I prepared for the next show and eased in to being a guest. Six months of practice later I was hosting my own show!

Managing your featured content

By clicking the + button in the feature area, you could add any of the following to the featured content area...

- A LinkedIn post.
- A LinkedIn article.
- A link to a blog post on some website.
- Media from your computer. For example a video or a PowerPoint presentation.

Click on the pencil button to manage your featured content – change the order, delete, add a comment, etc. Use # tags to increase your reach. Be sure to test that your chosen # tag is relevant – for example, #geographyteacher has 48 followers and #geography has 5766 followers.

Creating content to feature

Before you can feature something, you need to have something that you want to feature. You do that by clicking the *start a post* button. That's in both your activity area and at the top of your home screen. Here's some examples of content you might create...

- VIDEOS and PRESENTATIONS: Content that resides on your computer.

  Maybe you did a class or conference presentation that you're proud of? You could add a voiceover to it. Thinkific have a great blog post showing you how to do that.[32a] Be sure to talk about whats on the screen (interesting), rather than reading word for word off the screen (boring). Practice. Practice. Practice. That's the key to an interesting talk.

  Sound quality is important. Use a good microphone. If you can't borrow one, consider buying one. They're not expensive like they used to be. As a starting point search Google and YouTube for *usb podcast microphone review*. Record in an acoustically dull environment for best results. Surrounding yourself with bed covers or sleeping bags should be sufficient to achieve that.

- A POST: You write a post from your home screen. These are short. Maybe a couple of paragraphs long. You could paste a link to something and write a short comment explaining why you think its important. Use # tags here too.

- AN ARTICLE: You add an article in the start a post area at the top of your home screen. Articles can be much longer than posts – up to ~15,000 words. They are formattable with headings and can include photos and videos too. Use # tags here too.

32a Colin Burton, August 24 2020, How To Do A Voiceover On Google Slides Or PowerPoint, https://www.thinkific.com/blog/voice-over-powerpoint-or-google-slides/

People you may know (F)

This area displays a list of people you may know. The recommendations are based on things you have in common with other LinkedIn members. There are two parts to this...

1. The more complete your profile, and the more you participate in the LinkedIn platform, the more likely LinkedIn is to show you relevant suggestions. For example, people in your city who are also in your industry.

2. Look at the *people you may know* area in Figure 4 closely. It illustrates why it's important to fill in your LinkedIn profile correctly. Imagine that you're a hiring manager who's looking for an employee. Which of these three *people you may know* would you be inclined to click on? The one with a good headshot and crafted headline, or the two with no headshot and only token headlines?

Work experience (G)

The options here are all self-explanatory, except the *description* area. It is important to...

- **Quantify:** For example, *at [workplace] I developed a process that made [a weekly task] more efficient by 3 hours.*

- **Align yourself with brands if possible:** For example, *I worked for [workplace], a NASA preferred supplier.*

I talk about brand alignment and quantification when I show you how to write your résumé in part three. For the moment, fill this section in as best you can, and revisit it after you've completed the first draft of your résumé.

Education (H)

This is self explanatory. Click the plus button to add an education experience. As a student or recent graduate, you might choose to highlight aspects of courses you enjoyed or excelled at.

In the absence of workplace experience this is a great way to align yourself with an employer. For example, a software engineer graduate whose target industry sector is finance and knows that the sector's apps are mostly coded using the python language, might highlight the python component of their course...

- **Bad:** *I enjoyed coding and did well in my class project.*
- **Good:** *I enjoyed python coding most and I was awarded a high distinction for the currency trading app that I wrote.*

Skills and endorsements (I)

You add a new skill by clicking on the + button. LinkedIn will suggest a list of skills for you, and you can enter your own. Ideally the skills you add will be aligned with the job that you're targeting.

To help you decide which skills to add, refer back to the LinkedIn profiles you're using for inspiration. Notice which skills these people are being endorsed for. They're the skills that are important to their career, so it's likely they will turn up in a job's selection criteria. Could you be endorsed for those same skills? If not, could you somehow easily upgrade your skills so that you could be endorsed?

Some people will tell you to add as many skills as you can (LinkedIn allows fifty). This approach works well for search engines but can be overwhelming for humans. I think it gives a terrible impression. It can look like you're playing the system, is unlikely attract endorsements, and people are unlikely to scroll through it.

My advice is to carefully choose around 10-15 skills that align with your industry's expectations, and that you know colleagues will feel comfortable endorsing you for. Be sure to identify people who could endorse you and ask them to.

You delete or rearrange the order of your skills from the dialog that appears when you click the pen icon. Move your most important skills to the top so that they're easier to see. LinkedIn automatically organizes your skills into sections such as *industry knowledge, tools and technologies, and interpersonal skills.* Once you've added a skill, your first degree connections can click the + button next to it and endorse you.

You could also click the *take skill quiz* button and take a quiz. As with many things, the usefulness and value of these is questioned by some people. But, the good news is that they're not likely to do you any harm. When you're starting out, you need every bit of help you can get.

- Your results remain private until you choose to publish them.
- A result of 70% (pass score) or higher allows you to display a *verified skill* badge on your profile.
- You can only repeat a test once every three months.

Recommendations (J)

Ask your first degree connections to give you a recommendation. Maybe there's a lecturer, a boss from a part time job, or someone you've volunteered with who can do this?

Accomplishments (K)

Important things like publications, awards, language skills, etc.

Interests (L)

LinkedIn automatically populates this area based on groups you join, and businesses and institutions that you follow. Being a member of a relevant group confirms to an employer that you are *interested* in your industry (good). Contributing to a group confirms that you are a *participant* in your industry (better).

LinkedIn troubleshooting
What to say if you're unemployed?

Don't lie. Put an end date on your last job and list your current position as *open to opportunities*. Covid has left many people unemployed. It's also common for people to take gap years. Employers understand that. It's something to explain in an interview.

What if LinkedIn blocks you for exceeding search limits?

LinkedIn search limits change from time to time. If you're on the free plan (most people), you can get blocked for searching too much. But your stats are reset at the beginning of each month. If you're blocked, you can still search LinkedIn from Google and other search engines using x-ray search. You need to know a bit of code to do this. Google *x-ray search* to find detailed instructions on how to use it.

Here's three examples showing how to search for a python software engineer intern. To get the *site* part of an x-ray query right, you should find a couple of people relevant to you and look for patterns in the LinkedIn URL. Sometimes there's a country code prefix (hence *au* in the first example). Other times there seems to be either an */in/* or */pub/* URL suffix ...

- **Some have a country code:**
  site:au.linkedin.com/in/ intitle:intern python
- **Some have an /in/ suffix:**
  site:www.linkedin.com/in/ intitle:intern python
- **Some have a /pub/ suffix:**
  site:www.linkedin.com/pub/ intitle:intern python

More tips[33]...

- Log out of your LinkedIn account to get a full view of 3rd-degree contact profiles.
- X-ray search does not work as well with Google as it does with other search engines. You may need to try using Bing or Yahoo instead.

Why you should maintain your LinkedIn profile

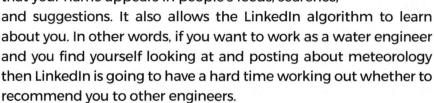

It's important to be active on LinkedIn. That ensures that your name appears in people's feeds, searches, and suggestions. It also allows the LinkedIn algorithm to learn about you. In other words, if you want to work as a water engineer and you find yourself looking at and posting about meteorology then LinkedIn is going to have a hard time working out whether to recommend you to other engineers.

You do not need to add content every day. But, say one to three times a week if you're in job search mode, and weekly to monthly if not. That's enough to demonstrate that you're interested in participating in your industry. You should continue to be active on LinkedIn throughout your professional life. The relationships you build there will make getting your next job, and the job after that, much easier.

---

33 Chirag Manghnani, X Ray Search LinkedIn – An Easy Way for Recruiters, https://www.geekyfy.com/x-ray-search-linkedin

Examples of content that you could add include slides of conference presentations, blog posts, and links to interesting relevant content that you come across. Be sure your content adds to the conversation and is not just for the sake of posting. Don't be like one fellow I'm linked with who treats LinkedIn like a teenager treats Facebook. He sometimes posts 3 times a day but is unable to answer questions about posts that he claims to be an authority on.

The important thing, especially when you're in networking and job seeking mode, is that when someone looks you up, they can get a flavor of the sorts of things that interest you, as well as your level of professionalism. The more active you are, the more visible you'll become.

Join and participate in industry groups. Post things that are relevant to your industry and comment on other people's posts. If you're active in groups, you'll be surprised at the number of relevant people will seek you out. A software engineer might post that there's been a recent code library update, or even write a review of the update. Someone else might post about a new widget that's about to hit the market. Both might comment on and add value to other people's posts.

Use hash tags to increase your reach. The greater your reach, the more likely your post is to be seen by someone who is relevant to you. To be sure that it's a hash tag that's being followed, type it into the LinkedIn search bar first. If no suggestions appear, then it's not a popular hash tag so you should try a different one. For example, #pythoncode is a LinkedIn suggestion but #pythoncodelibrary is not.

Posting thoughtful status updates shows that you have something to offer your industry. Employers can see these in your recent activity area. A switched on employer will see the benefit that an active LinkedIn group participant offers for their own brand building. Some may be keen to align themselves with you.

Develop a habit of being active on LinkedIn, and you'll have bigger and better networks than those who don't. That's a recipe for job and career opportunities, and it's also an insurance policy that gives you options if ever you are laid off.

PRESENCE PYRAMID LEVEL 3: Networking and building relationships

The intent of most networking is to build professional relationships and professional community, improve communication between organizations, and facilitate the exchange of ideas. The job market is not networking's primary purpose, but opportunities arise naturally for whoever makes the effort to be involved. Networking can seem insincere and manipulative, but it need not be.[34] The trick is to reframe it to be *relationship building*.

Networking seems to many of us to be an insincere way to manipulate relationships for personal gain. It is not if you do it properly.

Networking can take many forms. For example, a special event that's hosted by government, a corporate, or a professional organization. Networking can even take the form of a social event, or a corporate box at sports events. A business executive commented to me once...

Our corporate box lubricates my relationship with my clients. It means that if there's a problem, either of us can more easily pick up the phone and talk to each other, rather than picking up the phone and talking to our legal teams.

As is the case for business, relationships are important for job seekers because they lubricate the job seeking process. If you already have a relationship with someone, they're more likely to open their door and invite you in. But remember, as a job seeker, if its an employer who's opening their door, they're a person too. Just because they invite you over for coffee, that doesn't mean you want you to move in!

---

34 David Burkus, 2018, Friend of a Friend: Understanding the Hidden Networks That Can Transform Your Life and Your Career . HMH Books. Kindle Edition, Location 120

Jenni Gritters and Wudan Yan, are early career freelance writers. In their podcast episode called *Building Relationships*[35] they talk about how they (think *you*) use networking to build their writing businesses (think *get a job*). They also talk about how they (think *an employer*) respond to unsolicited requests for information or help. Spoiler alert. They're busy people who don't appreciate people wasting their time! That means, don't ask them (think *an employer*) about things that they already explain on their website. And don't cold email them and ask for access to their network. Why would they do that? They don't even know you! For a dose of tough love, you should take a half hour and listen to their episode.

Don't for a moment think that Jenni and Wudan's experiences are not relevant to you. They are 100% relevant. They are both successful jobbers. They're always pitching for work, so their job search skills are well honed. Networks are an essential ingredient to their success. More so than responding to advertisements.

So, how do Jenni and Wudan's experiences relate to you? Turns out there's a lot to be learnt from freelance journalists. Their podcast episode reinforces nearly everything I talk about in this book!

- **Understand your industry:** Wudan and Jenni both understand their industry. So do you since you researched your industry for the base of your *presence pyramid*.

- **Understand your target avatar:** Wudan and Jenni get work by making themselves relevant to the editors they're pitching to. When they pitch stories, they already know what type of stories the publication prints. They also know what an individual editor is likely to be receptive to, and they can show them similar stories that they've written in the past. You have a place to showcase your relevant interests and work too – your LinkedIn profile.

Unlike Jenni and Wudan's deep understanding of their clients, the avatars you have created are still too general. Networking will help you give your avatar's focus, but you may not yet have an established network. So read on...

---

35   Jenni Gritters and Wudan Yan, 2020 (May 4), The writers co-op episode 6, Building Relationships https://www.thewriterscooppod.com/episodes/buildingrelationships

---

Develop an elevator pitch

You need to develop an elevator pitch. A practiced, short, snappy, easy-to-grasp explanation of what you do, so named because you could say it to someone in the time it takes for an elevator ride.

There's all sorts of advice on how to write an elevator pitch. To be honest, most of the elevator pitches you'll find on the web read like B-grade marketing trash. Some people are okay with the likes of...

> *"I am a highly motivated and proactive sales manager, with outstanding networking and organizational skills. My keen ability to foster..." ...Yuk!*

That may be a good "starting point", but if you pitched that to me in an elevator... I'd run when it reached my floor. Nope. You wouldn't see me for dust!

The trick is to put yourself in an employer's boots. What type of pitch would you respond to? Imagine you're captain of a ball game or e-sport team. Would you feel inspired by the following elevator pitch... *I am a highly motivated and proactive goalie. I have outstanding teamwork and strategy skills. My keen ability to foster new players...* Probably not.

Keep your pitch short and concise. If you've been following my advice, you should have done sufficient industry research to know what will interest an industry professional.

For example, if as a software engineer graduate, you learn that there's a shortage of people who know about geographical code libraries, you'd be wise to do some research to upgrade your skillset. Your pitch at a networking event could go something along the lines of...

"I'm studying software engineering. Lately I've become fascinated by geographical code libraries."

"What do you mean by that?"

"Well, I've discovered that the [name of library] is really tricky because it allows you to do [some important thing that's relevant to an employer] that you couldn't do before."

"Gee, that's interesting. Tell me more."

"Well..."

I've heard recruiters say that they felt disappointed that they thought they had a personal conversation with someone, only to overhear them give the identical pitch to someone else. I can imagine that. But I also think that's an unavoidable danger when you're finding your feet. The base of your *presence pyramid* is not as wide as it is for someone who has years in your industry. You can avoid this problem by making your pitch short and interesting. If you deliver it with enthusiasm, it may just become a launching point for people to ask questions. Then you can move onto spontaneous conversation that's rooted in your deep knowledge of your topic area.

Examples of elevator pitches

What's your elevator pitch? I don't mean some B-grade marketer's rabble. I mean a genuine heartfelt sentence describing your career aspirations. There are some generic ideas on how to go about creating one. They include don't be too technical, don't be boring, don't be too long, make it conversational. Academic article writers have a great framework for this...

ACADEMIC TERM	ELEVATOR PITCH EQUIVALENT
Article title (~20 words)	Your elevator pitch
Abstract (100-300 words)	An *expanded elevator pitch* for someone who's interested in knowing more.
Article body (2000+ words)	The nuts and bolts of it. Reserve this for a long discussion with someone who's very interested in what you do.

You need to be able to say your elevator pitch and expand on it off the cuff. You should also be able to summarize it in case someone joins your conversation and they need to be brought up to speed. *I was just saying to Lou that I'm studying [subject] and really enjoying the [topic] part of it.*

There's two common formats for networking events. I've experienced both, but the second is the one that you're most likely to come across...

1. One where each attendee stands up and introduces themselves with their pitch.
2. One with a guest speaker who's followed by informal networking over drinks.

Here's how a networking conversation might go, followed by some examples of elevator pitches. Be sure to have your *expanded elevator pitch* in mind as well...

Hello. I'm Alex

I'm Lou

Pleased to meet you

What do you do Alex?...

*   *I'm studying cartography. At the moment I'm doing a habitat mapping project of an endangered critter for a local community group.*
*   *I love coffee and I'm studying to be a silver service barista.*
*   *I'm studying law. I'm fascinated by intellectual property and hope to specialize in entertainment IP.*
*   *I'm studying architecture. I'm doing an internship with a building company. Eventually I want to specialize in designing sustainable housing.*

You'll find more ideas by googling *elevator pitch examples [your job]*.

All the greats practice their pitches. So should you

Practice isn't the thing you do once you're good. It's the thing you do that makes you good.

The trick to a good elevator pitch is practice. Some of the most polished performances you'll ever see have their foundation in practice. For Malcolm Gladwell "Practice isn't the thing you do once you're good. It's the thing you do that makes you good."[36] Ever heard someone tell a hilarious joke, and then someone else tell the exact same joke, but it's not funny at all? Yes, it's true that there's people out there who could destroy any joke. Those people aside, often the difference between the two joke tellers amounts to practice.

The Archibald is a famous Australian art prize that's widely reported every year. In 2011, I interviewed one of the entrants, Ken Done, on live radio. Ken was, and still is, an Australian household name. During our interview, Ken wooed me with his off-the-cuff storytelling. The next day I heard him being interviewed on another radio station. His stories were identical to those he told me the day before...word-for-word.

Same for Tim Ferris. I started reading his 4 Hour Work Week after I heard him on the How I Built This podcast.[37] His interview was a mirror reflection of his book.

Steve Jobs of Apple fame was renowned for practicing his presentations.[38]

Ken Done, Tim Ferris and Steve Jobs were all so well practiced that it was impossible to tell that their interviews were scripted.

The lesson for you. Read your pitch aloud, and practice, practice, practice. With practice, comes the confidence to elaborate in a conversational way. Think of it as a mini college presentation. Be enthusiastic because enthusiasm is infectious. Role-play with friends and family. Reverse the role play. Role play different situations. For example, what if a new person enters the conversation. Practice is what professional sales teams do. They spend days on end role playing different scenarios with their colleagues. It's what Ken Done and Tim Ferris do, and Steve Jobs

---

36 Malcolm Gladwell, Outliers: The Story of Success, 2008, Penguin books.
37 GUY RAZ, December 21, 2020, How I Built This: Author and Podcaster: Tim Ferriss, https://www.npr.org/2020/12/18/948108821/author-and-podcaster-tim-ferriss
38 Carmen Gallo, January 12 2018, Steve Jobs Practiced 1 Habit That Turned Good Presentations Into Great Ones. The best CEO presenters follow one rule that made Steve Jobs a master showman, https://www.inc.com/carmine-gallo/steve-jobs-practiced-1-habit-that-turned-good-presentations-into-great-ones.html

---

did. That was an exhausting paragraph. It was intended to be. That's because practicing a pitch is exhausting.

Networking failure. Forgetting someone's name

A big failing of mine when I started to network was my inability to remember people's names. I'd get introduced to someone and once we started chatting, I'd get so consumed by the conversation that I'd forget the name of the person I was talking to. Not only was that embarrassing, it was almost guaranteed to make the other person feel unimportant. Here's some techniques that I use now...

1. Although I could use a spreadsheet or a diary, I create a contact for people I meet in my phone. I include where I know the person from, where they work, and other relevant information. That way, by searching my phone contacts I have multiple ways of finding and reminding myself about them.

2. When the situation allows it, I picture the person in my head and practice their name.

3. Sometimes I think of someone I already know who has the same name.

4. Before I attend an event, I reflect on the people I'm likely to see there. I picture their faces and recall their names.

5. If possible, I research likely event attendees before I go. That way, if I happen to meet them, I'm not ambushed by having to remember a new name.

6. I sometimes use a memory tool called a bestiary. More on that below.

Use a bestiary as a memory tool

I recently came across a useful technique for remembering names. In her memory craft book[39], Lynne Kelly writes that many memory champions started out with appalling memories, but improved when they learnt memory techniques.

Lynne's point is that people's names are often abstract. Names like Clementine, May, Clay and Rich are easy to remember

---

39 Lynne Kelly, 2019, Memory Craft: Improve your memory using the most powerful methods from around the world, especially chapter 1

---

because you can relate to them in some way. Few other names fall into this category.

Lynne uses a *bestiary* (a dictionary of beasts) as her memory tool. Then when she meets someone new she takes the first letters of their name and associates that with a beast. **Ca**trina might be associated with a **cat**, etc. Lynne suggests imagining the animal performing an action (the more dastardly the better), and revising your list of names regularly. For example, I recently met a fellow called **Os***car*. Now whenever I need to remember his name, I picture an **Os**trich driving a *car*.

If these ideas interest you then perhaps you could start by listening to a podcast interview on the Conversations hour on Australia's ABC radio.[40]

What to talk about when you network

Your aim when you network should be to get to know people so you can learn more about your industry, and if possible, tee up informational interviews (more on these later). Aim to get to know a few people well rather than a lot of people hardly at all.

You're not at a networking event to convince the person you're talking to that they should hire you. The old marketing example of someone bringing out an engagement ring on a first date applies here. Stop for a moment and think about that one... That's what asking for a job when you meet someone at an event equates to. Creepy don't you think?

Just be friendly and professional. Often, as a part of relationship building conversations, ideally with people who are doing the job you want to do, you'll get the opportunity to ask them about their job. The industry research you did for your *presence pyramid* should be sufficient to allow you to ask intelligent questions. You may also choose to draw on the style of questions I talk about in the informational interviewing section later in the book.

---

40 Also, Richard Fidler, June 3 2019, "The memory whisperer", Conversations podcast, https://www.abc.net.au/radio/programs/conversations/lynne-kelly-2019/11154756

Jenni Gritters and Wudan Yan showed us that there's a lot to learn about networking from freelance journalists. Taking the journalist theme further, veteran interviewers Malavika Varadan, Andrew Denton and Oprah have important things to say about talking to people.

In different ways, they each say that talking to people (think networking) *is not all about you.* Sure, you need an elevator pitch if you're asked about yourself. But, you need to be interested in other people too.

If you can't do small talk then you need to work on that. Small talk doesn't come naturally to everyone, but it is a skill that can be learnt. It's something that I never used to be good at. I was a farm boy, went to a boy's school, and entered a trade having just turned sixteen. I was absolutely unsocialized when I found myself at university in my 20s. I knew I had to get better at talking to people. I learnt by observing good communicators. Not so much people who talk about themselves all the time (although there's lessons to be learnt from the passion that self-talkers often ooze), but more so, people who were interested in other people.

Think about different occasions when you were talking with somebody, and how you felt afterwards. Some self-talkers have mastered the art of making you feel privileged to hear their stories. But, at the same time, they can also make you feel deflated if you don't think your stories compare to theirs. Contrast that to someone who's interested in you and what you have to say. They make you feel important just because they've taken the time to listen.

I got a lot better at small talk when I co-hosted a weekly interview hour on community radio. I was terrible when I started. I mean, really bad. But, I'm naturally interested in people, and I learnt how to ask questions and listen. And I took the time to observe skilled interviewers more closely.

You don't need to do a radio show to get good at talking to people. Having said that, it was the most important professional development that I've ever done. If you're game, find a friend and start a podcast or a community radio show on a topic you're passionate about. It's not only a great way to learn interviewing skills, it's also a great way to gain access to industry specialists who you otherwise wouldn't easily gain access to. Imagine having an excuse to telephone an industry leader with the following request ...

"Hello, its [your name] from [your industry] hour on Radio XYZ. Could you spare 10 minutes to talk to my listeners about [some aspect of] your work?"

There are plenty of free resources to help you get better at talking to people. For example, TED talks such as *7 ways to have a conversation with anyone* where the popular radio host Malavika Varadan (1.6m daily listeners) suggests skipping the small talk and asking appropriately personal questions.[41] [42]

I think that the most accessible way to get practice at small talk is to take a child or a dog for a walk. If you don't have one of your own, then offer to help someone out by baby sitting or doggy sitting. Doing that regularly has the potential not only to help you, but it can also morph into an act of generosity that enriches the lives of everyone who's involved.

Someone with a dog or a baby somehow feels like a safe person to talk to. Just this morning I saw both extremes of that. I made comment to a thirty-something year old woman about her dog. She gave me a *get away from me creep* look until my daughter and her new puppy appeared from out of the sun. The woman's face and body language instantly and visibly changed.

People with dogs and children are less reserved around other people with dogs and children. That's because your charge becomes a sort of walking character reference. You also have something in common with them. Parents and dog owners naturally talk to each other when their charges are playing together. What an ice breaker. I met lots of people as a dad with a young child, and again more recently when we got a family dog. I'm amazed at how easy

---

41 Malavika Varadan, "7 ways to have a conversation with anyone", https://www.youtube.com/watch?v=F4Zu5ZZAG7I
42 Find more relevant talks by googling the term *how to talk to people site:ted.com*

---

it's become for my normally shy 9 year old to talk to other dog owners about the new family puppy.

When you're out with your charge, observe the small talk. Study it. Practice it. In time, small talk will come more naturally to you.

Oprah says that all the people she has ever interviewed – Presidents, entertainers, prisoners – all they ever wanted to know was "*did you hear me, did you see me, and did I say anything that mattered?*"[43] She says...

- Listen 3 times more than you talk. Ask questions. Make eye contact. Frown. Nod. Respond non verbally. And, when you do talk, it should be to say something that is important to them, not you.

- Shine the spotlight on them. If you're meeting for the first time, offer a compliment. *Delighted to meet you, nice shirt,* ...

- Put away your stuff – your phone and other devices. Make them feel like they matter by giving them your full attention.

- Give. Help without being asked. Show that you care.

There's an important clue in Oprah's observation on giving. Most professional organizations have committees that organize newsletters, meetings, conferences, etc. Offer to help. Contact the committee. Tell them that you're keen to get involved in your profession's community, and that you're available to help. You'll get to know other industry people on the committee, and by knowing them, your conversations will come easier and be more relaxed. And you'll have the chance to demonstrate that you're a capable and intelligent worker. Be prepared to do jobs like taking minutes, setting up for meetings, meeting and greeting at events, and communicating with members for various reasons.

As PhD students, my life partner and her friends joined their peak professional body and became committee members – alongside

---

43 Jeff Haden, Oprah Winfrey Says Answering 1 Question Lets You Give Anyone You Meet the Most Important Gift of All, https://www.inc.com/jeff-haden/oprah-winfrey-says-answering-1-question-lets-you-give-anyone-you-meet-most-important-gift-of-all.html

---

numerous senior industry and government people. They helped organize a national conference where they got to meet industry players who they otherwise wouldn't have met. Their names were synonymous with the event.

In my mind, Andrew Denton is one of the best long form interviewers in the world. He attributes the success of his in-depth interviews to the quality of his questions. These are seeded by careful research and then attentive listening to the person he's interviewing.[44]

In his interview with Michael Stipe from REM, Andrew makes an amazing effort to evoke Michael's memory. A prop he brings out from Michael's past seems to almost shock him. Watch and see how the interview becomes more intimate. It's a terrible quality recording, but worth looking at just to observe how generosity can affect relationships.[45]

Search YouTube for longform interviewers like Andrew Denton, Oprah and others. Watch closely and analyze how they go about their job. Study them. Read transcripts if they're available. Notice that they ask questions that demonstrate genuine interest and then they mostly listen. People who listen have a better chance of leaving a good impression. The opposite is true for those who don't.

I was once in the same social circle as a state politician. He'd always approach me with a smile and shake my hand. We'd make small talk, but he never remembered my name. As we talked, his eyes would be scanning the room, I always assumed for someone more important to talk to. He was renowned for that. The point to this story is that its years since I've seen this politician. His name and his bad behavior are the *only* memory I have of him!

---

44 Chris Ashmore, Lessons From A Veteran Interviewer: Andrew Denton On Game Changers, Δ40

45 Andrew Denton michael stipe interview part 2 https://www.youtube.com/watch?v=EObsPalz9Wk&t=220s

---

How to network on LinkedIn

There are two ways to put yourself on the radar for new LinkedIn connections. They are via it's search engine and via its relationship engine.

- **LinkedIn's search engine is like google:** The LinkedIn search engine looks for keywords to return results relevant to a search term. That's why I spent time showing you how to create keyword rich searchable headings when we created your profile.

- **LinkedIn's relationship engine is like Facebook:** LinkedIn's relationship engine uses your connections to make connection suggestions. It also matches your professional interests to other people's interests, and where you live to where other people live. Like Facebook, the more active you are, the more likely you are to get more numerous, more relevant and better quality connections.

This section is about the magic of LinkedIn's relationship engine. When you're connected to someone in an organization, the relationship engine is what suggests you as a connection for other people in the same organization. That includes recruiting staff. That's a big incentive to complete your LinkedIn profile and make connections!

But, having lots of connections is a *vanity measure*. Unless you want to be a LinkedIn influencer, you should aim for a modest number of career relevant connections. That's a *victory measure!*

Join LinkedIn groups. Not only does your membership of the group display in your LinkedIn interests area, it also gives you the ability to message other group members, and improves your chances of turning up in their *people you may know* area.

When you reach out to connect with someone. Never send a *Hi, I'd like to join your LinkedIn Network*, or any other prepopulated LinkedIn request. It reeks of laziness. That's not the impression you want to give.

Like many busy people, I reject most prepopulated LinkedIn invitations outright. For people who approach me with a relevant personalized message, the more their profile tells me about them, the easier it is for me to imagine how they might be relevant to me. In less than 30 seconds I can see how much of their profile is filled in, how active they are, and what groups they're in.

Your connection request should be personalized and reflect that you know the reason why you want to connect with them. Busy people do not have time to consider anything other than meaningful requests (remember what Wudan Yan and Jenni Gritters said about that[46]). Maybe you've read an article they wrote, read their comments in a group discussion, or you simply came across their profile and found it interesting.

So, before writing a connection invitation to someone, study their LinkedIn profile, and google their name to look for blog posts, interviews, and videos about them. That will allow you to write a (max 299 character) personalized connection invitation that's more likely to be accepted.

You will find your own style for connecting with people. Googling "examples of personalized LinkedIn invitations" will return lots of results. Find examples that resonate with you and then alter them to make them your own. Following are some ideas ...

- *Dear [name]. We're both in the [group name] LinkedIn group. I really enjoyed your post today about [topic]. Please connect so that I can keep in touch and learn more about your work. Regards, [your name]*

- *Dear [name]. I came across [article name] and looked you up on LinkedIn. That's the focus of my studies at [university]. Please accept my invitation to connect with you so that I can follow your work. Regards, [your name].*

- *Dear [name]. It was great to meet you at [event name]. I enjoyed our chat about [topic]. Please accept my invitation to connect. Regards, [your name].*

- *Dear [name]. I'm a recent graduate in [degree]. I'd like to learn more about your work and career and would really appreciate connecting with you Regards, [your name].*

46 Jenni Gritters and Wudan Yan, 2020 (May 4), The writers co-op episode 6, Building Relationships https://www.thewriterscooppod.com/episodes/buildingrelationships

Networking in person

Networking can happen anywhere with anybody. Whenever you're talking to somebody, anybody, don't be afraid to tell them what you're doing. If you don't tell people what you're doing, how are they meant to find out? Let me say that again because it really is important. You need to have a go at getting over your shyness. Of getting over your imposter syndrome. *If you don't tell people what you're doing, how are they meant to find out?*

Years ago, a new neighbor seemed interested in my soil mapping work. Turns out she was an engineer at a water utility. They had been struggling to find a link between soils and bursting water pipes. Later that week I began a new line of work in my business.

It never fails to amaze me how simply mentioning what you're doing to someone can lead you to opportunity. They might know someone who's relevant to you. In the pull-quote, I tell the story about how I once gained a major client following a chat to a new neighbor.

This next story illustrates why you should always be polite and acknowledge people you're in a group with. You never know who they might be.

A friend of a friend is a huge formula 1 racing fan. At a dinner event, he managed to sit on the same table as his F1 hero. He became annoyed with George, the fellow sitting next to him. Every time he started a conversation with his hero, George would interrupt. As he was leaving the event, he sparked up a polite conversation with George.

"What do you do George?"

"I'm retired now. But I used to play in a band."

"Would I know it?"

"Maybe... The Beatles."

And then there's Bobbi Brown. She built a famous makeup brand in the 1980s.[47]

After graduating from college, Bobbi got her first shot as a makeup artist after writing to a freelancer with a request to be her assistant. That was her start. She met her industry, occasionally worked in TV, and hustled by showing her portfolio to as many people as she could. The relationships Bobbi built while doing low paying work helped her get better paying work.

Chatting to a chemist one day, Bobbi complimented him on the store's cosmetics line. He made them himself. Her first manufacturer!

Another time she mentioned that she made cosmetics to someone at a party. The woman was a cosmetics buyer for a luxury department store. Orders followed.

Bobbi met her next manufacturer in an elevator.

And best of all. After a store appearance, a little old lady asked if there was anything she could do to help Bobbi's business. Jokingly, Bobbi said, *I don't know. I'd love to be a regular on the Today Show.* The little old lady replied, *Honey... The executive producer is my grandson.*

My point in giving you these glimpses into Bobbi's story is to show you how getting out there and telling people what you're doing, allows opportunities to present themselves. Also, I wanted to show you that sometimes low paying jobs present opportunities to build relationships that can lead to better paying jobs.

Get a friend or family member to introduce you

But what if you think you don't know anyone worth networking with? Maybe you do without realizing it. You're going to have to be resourceful.

Networks are a way for employers to prequalify you for interview. So, make sure that you let as many people as possible know that

---

47 Guy Razz, How I built this podcast, Bobbi Brown Cosmetics: Bobbi Brown (2018), July 19 2021, https://npr.org/2021/07/16/1016898855/bobbi-brown-cosmetics-bobbi-brown-2018

---

you're looking for a new job. Many recruiters will meet a candidate who is referred to them by someone they know.[48]

Most jobs aren't advertised, and some employers may be too busy to post job openings. Friends and family are great at looking out for these types of jobs because they care. They're more likely to be proactive in contacting their network to find opportunities for you. And they will often praise you to a prospective employer, further increasing your chances of getting the job.[49] Within my network, I did this for a friend only yesterday (and she got the job).

But you have to do your bit too. People are more likely to feel good about recommending you if they can verify for themselves that you're a good choice. A good LinkedIn profile makes their job easier. It allows them to send an employer your profile link and so be able to say more than *I've known them since they were little.* Fame works at the micro-scale too. Given the chance, few people will miss an opportunity to attach themselves to it. It's a form of status to be able to recommend someone who's likely to become a valuable employee.

Never underestimate someone because you know them socially. They could have a very different working life. If someone you know offers to introduce you to someone they know, prepare for your meeting in the same way you would if you had sought that person out and organized the meeting yourself. I say that because I blew it once.

When I was a fourth year student, a family friend setup an informational interview for me with one of his colleagues. I was surprised that the loud office chatter quelled when the family friend greeted me in his work's foyer. I didn't know that he was the second most senior person in the 20,000+ member organization! I didn't perform very well. I dressed inappropriately and failed to do any research on the workplace before I went. Granted, that sort of research was not so easy in the early 1990s. But had I prepared

---

48   What percent of jobs that are filled are not posted publicly?, https://www.quora.com/What-percent-of-jobs-that-are-filled-are-not-posted-publicly

49   Andrea Workman, 2012, What percent of jobs that are filled are not posted publicly?, https://www.quora.com/What-percent-of-jobs-that-are-filled-are-not-posted-publicly

---

for the meeting, with his endorsement, who knows what direction my career could have taken?

Talk to people outside your immediate circle of family and friends as well. *Birds of a feather flock together* goes the old saying, so tight circles can sometimes be limiting. Your plumber friends might all be domestic plumbers and not know commercial plumbers. Barista friends might all work in cafes and not big hotels. Lawyer friends might all be commercial lawyers and not family lawyers. Engineer friends might all work on oil rigs and not for local government. Software engineer friends might work in the finance sector but not in the manufacturing sector,...

Family friends, school friends, and neighbors that you don't see day to day are some examples of people outside your immediate circle. Friend of a friend is a topic all of its own. Big enough for David Burkus to write a book about. You guessed it, its called *Friend of a friend*.[50]

Ask people in your inner circle if they know anyone who might be relevant to you. For example, an email might go...

Dear cousin Sam. I'm close to finishing my degree in [topic]. I'm looking for people who are currently working as a [job]. I want to speak to them so I can find out more about both the job and the industry. Do you know anyone who you could introduce me to? Thanks. [your name]

Here's an example of how a chat with someone at a party might go...

How's your day been going?

Great thank you.

What have you been up to?

I've been researching what its like to be a [job]. I'm about to start looking for [people who do that job] to talk to about it.

My uncle does that.

Do you think he'd talk to me? If I give you my details, would you could contact me if he agrees?

---

50 Burkus, 2018, Friend of a friend, Houghton Mifflin Harcourt

Contact peak bodies and professional organizations to find networking events

People working in peak bodies are likely to be helpful because that's their job. Often peak bodies have special categories of memberships for students and early career professionals. Many offer things like mentor programs, conferences and conference grants, and networking events. You may need to join to access these benefits.

To find your local peak body, google terms like...

[job/industry] [peak body/association/organization]
[your location]

"software engineer" "peak body" "New York"

Web research can sometimes return upcoming events. Sites like eventbright.com and meetup.com are good for this. If you can't find any, contact the peak body and ask if they've forgotten to add them to their website. Be sure to write down the name of the person you spoke to. Assuming you've been courteous, you've possibly just added someone to your network. Someone who now has a tiny personal investment in you. Often that's enough for them to make sure you're introduced around at the next networking event. The people who staff peak bodies are the ones with their ear to the ground. Some will even look out for opportunities for you.

Not many job seekers think to look for help from peak bodies. Philanthropic organizations, college career centers, and college faculties are worth trying too. They can steer you to events, opportunities and employers. Some also have grants that you may be able to access to attend networking events such as conferences. Start with their website before you contact them. The competition for these grants is sometimes small. I once congratulated an early career academic for having won so many. His response... *Nobody seems to realize that the grants and awards are there. Often I win them because I'm the only one who applied for them.*

Research who's likely to attend a networking event

Some industries have regular networking events and others don't. You need to make the most of those events when they occur.[51] You do that by finding out who attended previous events, who sponsors the event, and who'll be presenting at the next event. Then, with the aid of LinkedIn, you compile a list of people to target – specifically, people whose expertise aligns with your interests. Magically, it's easier to enter into conversations with people who you have things in common with. Networking events become far more enjoyable and rewarding that way.

Professional sales people always know who'll be attending an event, who they want to talk to, and what they want to talk to them about. What sales people do is relevant to you as a job seeker because, like it or not, you're selling something too – you!

When you're chatting to someone, in addition to the sorts of topics I touch on in the informational interviewing section later in this book, there's plenty of things you could talk about. For example, an interesting presentation you attended at the event, them, and of course, yourself. Do not ignore late career people. They're often done with career building and many are in mentoring mode. They tend to know lots of people, have their colleague's respect, and many will be proactive in introducing you around.

Here's the research you should do before an event...

Event sponsors:

- Which businesses regularly attend the functions?
- What type of work does each business do?
- Of the businesses that are relevant to you, who are they likely to send along and what's their job? Find them on LinkedIn and study their profiles.

---

51 Some are expensive, so look for grants from peak bodies and professional organizations. Plan ahead because you may need to be a presenter rather than just an attendee in order to qualify.

Event attendees: Often lists of attendees are published on the day of the event. You may not know the attendees this time, but you can use the list to research them for next time.

Event speakers: Most events publish a list of speakers. For events with lots of speakers, use the free Chrome extension *instant data scraper*[52] to automatically extract a spreadsheet file from the speaker list page. That will make the data easier for you to manage.

At first glance, the idea of researching event participants may seem a little creepy. Let me illustrate why it's not. Years ago, I presented a model for understanding water pipes failures at an international infrastructure conference. Infrastructure can be anything from water pipes, to roads, to nuclear submarines and rocket ships. There were around 2000 attendees from all sorts of industries at the conference, so it was important for me to find delegates who were in the water industry. The question that arises is *how do you research event participants?* Well, LinkedIn is your friend!

Prior to the event: Introduce yourself on LinkedIn. Mention that you'll be at the same event and would like to catch up.

> *... hello [person's name]. My name is [your name]. I came across your name when I was researching the upcoming [event name]. I'm a [field of study] student and I was hoping to meet you at the event and ask you about your job*

After the event: You could request an informational interview...

> *Hello [person's name]. My name is [your name]. I was hoping to bump into you at [event name] last night. I'm a [field of study] student and I wanted to ask you about your job. Could you spare 20 minutes to talk with me? Would you allow me to buy you coffee somewhere near your work? Or I could come to your office. Whichever you prefer.*

In person at the event: Because, prior to the event you looked at their LinkedIn profile, after introducing yourself...

> *...and what do you do?*

---

52 Instant Data Scraper – Chrome Web Store (google.com), https://webrobots.io/instantdata

---

I work for [company name]...

Then you could say... I've heard of them. Don't they do [some type of work]?...

Present a paper at the event: Sometimes people will approach you afterwards. For example, after my presentation at the infrastructure conference, the chair of the International Water Association sought me out.

Another way to find workplaces that might be hiring

Be realistic when you look for places to work. There is nothing wrong with wanting to land a trophy job at a business like google. But know that the competition for jobs at trophy workplaces is fierce compared to similar jobs in other workplaces. For example, in the US, there's over 40,000 searches each month for *google intern*, compared to around 10,000 searches for *software engineer intern*.[53] But in 2019, google employed <1% of the tech workforce in the US.[54] In other words, there's four times the number of searches for intern opportunities offered by a business that employs <1% of the tech workforce! Unless you're a superstar, you're better off looking for work in smaller, growing workplaces. They're more likely to be in hiring mode than mature businesses anyhow.

Google *fastest growing businesses in [location name]* (e.g. fastest growing businesses in America) to find websites that identify these businesses. Here's two websites that you should look at.

inc.com: Every year Inc publishes its list of fastest growing private companies for America. You can refine the list by industry, state, city and number of times the company has appeared on the list. Google "*Inc's List of Fastest Growing Private Companies*" to find the most recent list.

---

53 Google keywords tool

54 Calculation ((google tech/all US tech)*100) is an approximation because the statistics are from different times in the year. Sources follow...
   google tech: Alphabet: Number of Employees, https://www.macrotrends.net/stocks/charts/GOOG/alphabet/number-of-employees
   All US tech: N.F. Mendoza, April 21 2020, US tech industry had 12.1 million employees in 2019, https://www.techrepublic.com/article/us-tech-industry-had-12-1-million-employees-in-2019

Fast growing companies: Look for fast growing companies on your country's stock exchange. *Small Caps* (<$2b value and typically with employee numbers in the low hundreds) are more likely to be in growth mode than *large caps* (>$10b value and typically with many thousands of employees). Google *small caps [your country name]* and explore the results, especially news sites. Look for headlines that indicate a company might be growing. When you find one, google *[company name] report*.

As an example, after 10 minutes of research, I found an Australian technology small cap called Audinate. I googled "Audinate report" and found its *First Half 2021 Results Report*. In the report I found the following dot point...

- *Video development team of 11 staff recruited in Cambridge, more to come.*

That statement led me to check the Audinate web site where I found 10 jobs advertised, PLUS a special job category with the description.

> *We're always looking for talented for people to join our global team. If you don't see the right role listed below but believe you have the right skills to make a difference at Audinate, let us know...*

But wait. There's more! On its site, Audinate has lots of information about its products. It even has a free certificate program. The certificates are a fantastic resource for electrical engineers and sound engineers to upgrade their résumé and LinkedIn profile. That would make them a more attractive employee prospect, if not to Audinate, then to a manufacturer who uses Audinate chips (e.g. Yamaha, Sony, Bose, Bosch, Roland, ...), or to a business that uses gear with Audinate chips in it (e.g. TV stations, events businesses, ...).

Not many business websites have an Audinate style open invitation to apply, but they do exist, and they're more likely to be found on the websites of growing businesses. Informational interviews are a good way to find businesses that are likely to be receptive to you. I talk about informational interviewing in the next section.

Do informational interviews to understand a job and build networks

Informational interviews are exactly that. They're there to fill gaps in your knowledge about a job. You use the information you gather to improve your LinkedIn profile, your résumé, and as a trigger to do additional (low cost/free) training that will make you more attractive to an employer. Informational interviews are not about getting a job. If you view them like that you are in danger of coming across as insincere and manipulative. Akin to the marketing example I gave earlier of producing an engagement ring on a first date (creepy!).

Some interviewees are easier to find than others. For example, it's easy to meet hospitality workers so long as you pick a quiet time of day to ask. Understanding the rhythms of your industry should be a part of your job research anyhow. Here's how you might approach someone... *Hi, I'm Alex. I'm thinking of starting a career as [job] in the hospitality industry. Could you spare some time to talk to me about what the job is like?*

Same goes for accountants. End of financial year is not a good time to seek informational interviews with them.

There's no shortage of people on LinkedIn that you could request informational interviews from. You could target an employer in the exact industry and location you want to work.

There's significant numbers of LinkedIn members in almost any profession you can name, including hospitality and trades. For example, in my 5 million population city, there's > 150,000 each of accountants, software engineers and marketers. You can send connection requests to anyone who's a member of a group you're in (so join relevant groups), or a 3rd degree contact or less.

If you're not having success getting people to respond to your LinkedIn requests, then maybe they're not monitoring their LinkedIn account. It might be time to look for their contact details and call them. There's a script for that towards the end of this section.

When someone is generous enough to give you their time, you should respect it by having a list of questions to ask. Write your questions down on paper and leave space for taking notes under each one. There's nothing wrong with this. Watch current affairs hosts. Its common for them to refer to their notes.

Take Oprah's advice and put your devices away! Turn your phone off or put it into airplane mode. Be attentive and professional. Don't get a reputation as a timewaster. Don't blow this. It may only be an information gathering exercise, but it is also an opportunity to make yourself known to someone in your industry. It's an opportunity to build a personal connection in a way that's not intimidating to the person you're talking to, and may lead to more introductions.

Use *open questions*. Open questions are questions that are hard to give *yes* or *no* answers to. For example...

- *What are the best parts of the job?* NOT *Are there any really good parts of the job?*
- *What are the worst parts of the job?* NOT *Are there any bad parts of the job?*
- *As someone who supervises early career [job], what could they do to make your job easier?* NOT *Is there anything that would make your job easier?*

Other questions might go along the lines of...

- *How did you find your way into this job? What are the paths that your colleagues have taken that have led them to the same place as you?*
- *What tasks did you do when you first started out?*
- *What skillsets are new graduates likely to lack that would make...*
  - their job easier.
  - them more valuable.

As for an exhaustive list of informational interview questions to ask, google the term *"informational interview questions" [your job]*. My suggestion is to finalize your questions after you are comfortable that you've done a good job of your industry research, and after you have researched both the person you'll be interviewing and the business they work in. Limit the number of questions so that your interview only lasts around 20 minutes. Most people are busy and don't have time for meetings that last longer than that.[55]

Sometimes the person you interview will mention a colleague's name. Assuming their colleague is relevant to you, and the interview is going well, don't be afraid to say something along the lines *do you think [colleague name] would mind if I contact them?* Your interviewee's response will guide you how to use that information. Sometimes they may offer to introduce you to them.

Being given a name to ask for allows you to warm call somebody else. In the following example, it would be unlikely that Alex would get past reception in the absence of a referral. Here's what I mean ... Imagine that Alex has met Kim for coffee. Kim suggests that an old colleague Lou at ABC Co might be someone else Alex should speak to. Here's how Alex would go about that...

- **Via ABC Co switchboard:**

  Hello. My name is Alex. I'd like to speak to Lou please ...

  pause ... *May I ask what its about?*

  Yes, an old colleague of Lou's, Kim, suggested that we should speak

  ... pause while switchboard calls Lou... *Putting you through...*

- **Direct line:** *Hello. Is that Lou?*

  ... Speaking ...

  My name is Alex. Kim from AAA Co suggested that I should talk to you. ...

  How's Kim? ...

  Very well ...

  How can I help you Alex? ...

  Well, I'm doing some research to understand what it might be like to work as a [job name], and also trends that might be happening in the [industry name]. Last week Kim talked to me

---

55 Nathan Perez and Marcia Ballinger, 2014, The 20-Minute Networking Meeting – Graduate Edition: Learn to Network. Get a Job, Career Innovations Press.

---

about what its like to be a [job] over coffee. I was wondering if you might be able to spare 20 minutes for a short chat too? Would you allow me to buy you coffee somewhere near your work? Or I could come to your office. Whichever you prefer. ...

- *Sure. Make an appointment at an agreed meeting place (perhaps suggest a café that you googled before you telephoned). Be sure to respect the Lou's time and stick to the agreed 20 minutes.*

- *No. I can't do that. But I can spare you some time now. Thank Lou and then briefly ask your questions. If you think the interview has gone well, finish by asking... Could you suggest someone else who might have the time to talk to me?*

- *No. I'm too busy for that ... That's okay. Could you suggest a colleague who might have the time to talk to me?*

If the subject of employment comes up, pursue the conversation if you really want to. Otherwise, you might choose to say something along the lines of *at this stage I'd like to finish my research so I can understand where I fit in. Would you mind if I contact you again after I've completed that?*

Be sure to send a short thank you note afterwards.

The importance of a thank you note

Thank you notes are not only good manners, they're also an excuse to make contact with the person who interviewed you. If it's a follow up to a job interview, it's a chance to remind them why you're interested in the position. Beyond that, thank you notes demonstrate your professionalism. They send a subtle message that if you were to work in that workplace, that's how you'd treat your colleagues and clients. It's also an opportunity to remind the person that you're there, and to confirm your contact details with them, including a link to your awesome LinkedIn profile that you happened to update to reflect what you discussed in your informational interview. The following short letter does all that...

Alex Johnson,
Ph: 123 456 789
Email: Alex@SomeDomain.com

Lou Woodyard
XYZ Company
Email: Lou@SomeDomain.com

[Date]

Dear Lou

Thank you for your time yesterday. I enjoyed our chat. You really helped me gain a better understanding about what it would be like work as a [job]. I shall keep you posted as my career research matures.

Kind regards,
Alex Johnson

linkedin.com/in/alex-johnson-geographer

You want to build champions for you cause. That means that anyone who helps you (even the helpful receptionist) should get a thank you note. Something as simple as...

Dear [name]. Thanks so much for talking to me yesterday. I really appreciate the advice you gave me, and the time you took to do it. Kind regards. [your name].[56]

The recruiting community complain that hardly anybody does this. Put yourself in the other persons shoes. How would you feel? I know I always feel a bit used when I take the time to help someone, and then never hear from them again. Or, even worse, when you do hear from them again, they want something else.

Excuses to make contact are a common tactic used by sales teams. They use them because they work. I used to know the manager of a national transport company. He told me the story of a client who had lots more business, but would not take his sales calls. Then one day, a

---

56 Bolles, Richard N., 2020, What Color Is Your Parachute? 2020, p.133, Potter/Ten Speed/Harmony/Rodale. Kindle Edition.

nervous forklift driver knocked on my friend's office door. One of the client's pallets had been damaged by a forklift. Rather than chastising the staff member, much to the forkie's relief, my friend thanked him.

My friend called his client and apologized (note that the client took his call this time). He then fast tracked the insurance claim, and as an apology, invited the client to see his favorite football team play from a corporate box the following week. Guess what? They built a relationship and more business was done!

Some people suggest sending a gift along with a thank you note. To be honest, that doesn't sit well with me. I think it changes the dynamic. It turns a favor into a transaction. It can also offend if the thoughtfulness of the gift undervalues the recipients time. My call is that unless it is a culturally required practice to send thank you gifts, then don't. But if you do want to give something, then make sure the gift is a thoughtful (but not necessarily expensive) one. Google *small gift ideas* and plenty of ideas come up. For example, a tea infuser with loose leaf tea.

If you look around the web, there's hundreds of examples of thank you note templates. Many are nauseatingly saccharine! Yuk! Either use one of the two examples above, or find one you like on the web. But, be sure to make it your own before you use it. As a guide, never say anything in a thank you note that you wouldn't say to someone in person. You risk coming across as false if you do. A good test for that is to read your note aloud. If it sounds nauseatingly saccharine, then it probably is!

Finally, when you get a job, send a thank you note to everyone who helped you along the way. Its not just good manners, it's a way to build and maintain the relationship that you've started – relationships that might grow into friendships, or at least continue to be important once your career is underway.

Employers like to try before they buy

Different employers have different strategies for employing people.

A low risk way for employers to test if you're a good fit for their workplace is to hire you for small jobs. That way, if you don't work out then they don't have to fire you. Employers can just say that the project has ended without having to worry about wrongful dismissal claims. It works both ways. Small jobs are also chance for you to test if that workplace is right for you.

Employing the right people is so important to Zappos that it has a unique one-month onboarding process. At the end of the onboarding month Zappos may or may not offer ongoing employment. All recruits are offered one month's pay as an incentive to leave if they feel that Zappos is not for them.[57] For Zappos, that ensures that only people who really want to work for them stay.

You're rarely competing for ongoing work when employers are trying before buying. You just need to do all you can to give them the confidence to take the next step and employ you full time. That's why it's important that you work onsite as much as possible. In the business world, corporate consultants regard working onsite as *business building*. In your case, its an opportunity for you and an employer to get to know each other, and for you to dazzle them with the quality of your work and your professionalism!

Here's some examples of "try before you buy" from my working life...

- As a school boy, I had a part time job cleaning silverware in an antique shop. That employer later found me an apprenticeship as an antique furniture restorer.
- As a university student, I did a research project within a government mapping department. After a couple of months, I was offered a full time job (that I politely rejected).
- As a postgraduate student I worked part time for one of my professors. He won a grant and when I graduated, he offered me a full time job (that I gratefully accepted).
- And in my consulting life... one project often led to another, and another, and another.

---

57 Hollie Delaney, November 20, 2019, Zappos gives new employees 4 weeks to decide if it's a good fit — and lets them quit with pay if not. Their head of HR explains how this policy has helped them save money and hire great people, https://www.businessinsider.com.au/zappos-head-of-hr-four-weeks-onboarding-hire-great-people-2019-11

PART THREE
– How to apply for a job

PARALLEL UNIVERSE #3
– AFTER ALEX HAS FINISHED READING THIS BOOK.

Industry research complete – check! Workplace research and avatars complete – check! LinkedIn profile reflects all Alex's research and the chat with Lou at last month's networking event – check! Job application addresses all the criteria in the job description – check!

Lou is overworked and understaffed. The right employee would take the pressure off. The responses from last week's ad keep coming in. Over two hundred already. Evaluating them is another job on top of everything else. It wouldn't be so bad if they were all killer candidates, but so far, they all seem hell-bent on sabotaging their chances. None have made the effort to address the carefully crafted job description, so only a few have made it into the *maybe* pile.

Returning from a break, Lou sits down to check more emails. *Spam, spam, spam, spam. Oh. Here's one. My new employee perhaps? Bla, bla, bla...promising...résumé attached...hmmm...*

Let's compare this to the job description. Yes, yes, yes. Hmmm.

Friendly cover letter. Résumé meets all the selection criteria. Interned at [a business Lou knows well]. Increased revenue stream by 5%. Hmmm ... Ahhh ... There's a LinkedIn profile. Let's look at that... Hmmm ... Impressive. Status updates ... Yes... Friendly photo... Friendly photo... Friendly photo... That's it. I know Alex. We had a long chat at last month's networking meet. Hooray. Let's invite Alex in for a chat!

The work you've put into your *presence pyramid* will make writing your job application easier, higher quality and more effective than it otherwise would have been.

The challenge is to demonstrate to an employer that you're interested and engaged. That you have something to offer and that you can be trained. You achieve that by taking the avatars you created in part two, one step further by researching the business you're applying to and tailoring your application to a job description. Your LinkedIn profile is there to reinforce your application. With any luck, the relationships you've been nurturing mean that the job you're applying for is with someone you already know.

That's right. You don't send the exact same résumé out to hundreds of different employers. Unfocussed job applications are doomed to fail. I received lots of boilerplate résumés and cover letters when I owned my environmental mapping consultancy. Few applications I received ever mentioned the software I used, and fewer still mentioned an interest in environmental mapping. So, 1) irrelevant software and 2) no interest in the type of work I did. What are the chances that I would show any interest? Z E R O!!!

Point made? You need to customize each job application to each workplace! It's a lot of work. You may not want to do it. But what makes you think an employer would want to read an irrelevant application? That they will care enough to draw the links between your résumé and their requirements? Nobody ever said that getting a job was easy!

Remember the avatars you created in part two? In this section, we'll update them and give them focus on the job you're applying for. Don't worry. It's not nearly as big a task as last time. They will feed into your *presence* so that you can present yourself as someone who already knows the software, systems, problems, and products that make up a hiring manager's workplace. Someone who will be productive quickly and require minimal training is a tempting double-whammy for an employer. That's what will set you apart from other candidates and reduce the friction for hiring you.

PRESENCE PYRAMID LEVEL 4: How to research a workplace

So, you've found a job that you want to apply for. Now you need to check that its a workplace you'd like to work in. There's nothing worse than being stuck somewhere you don't like. You need to be sure that you'll be doing the sort of work that you like to do. That its a workplace where you can reach your potential. And that the business' values align with yours.

Search LinkedIn for the workplace's past and present employees. Typically, how long do people work there for? Lots of long term employees suggests a happy workplace with deep corporate knowledge, and hopefully a culture of mentorship. Excepting startups, lots of short term employees can mean the opposite.

Search Q&A sites like Reddit, Stack Exchange and Quora, as well as employer review sites such as those listed in Table 3. Sometimes google returns better results than a Q&A site's search engine. So, try googling *[workplace name] site:[Q&A site name]* (e.g. ABC-co site:quora.com). On sites that give employers a score, dig deep enough to be sure that the score relates to the role you're interested in. For example, a low score for a transport company might reflect consistently low scores by a large number of drivers that masks consistently high scores by small number of office staff.

If you're satisfied with your research, it's time to give the avatars you created in part two focus on the job you want to apply for. Either print the avatars out so you can write notes on them, or copy them so you can modify the copied versions digitally.

Advertised jobs should be accompanied by a job description. Download it. Some job descriptions are more detailed than others. If you're pitching for an unadvertised position, try finding historical job descriptions for the workplace using the techniques I showed you for industry research in part two. You might need to give the queries I showed you there, focus on the workplace with the job. Try googling...

- [workplace name] [job] "position description" (e.g. "Home Depot" "marketer" "position description")
- "job description" site:[workplace website] (e.g. "job description" site: homedepot.com)

Now continue your research. You're looking for any insights into the job or the workplace that you can find. Look up the business, the hiring manager and, if it's an existing role, the person already doing your job on LinkedIn and google. Sometimes you can be lucky.

Google search...
- [hiring manager name] Interview (e.g. Lou Woodyard interview)
- [workplace name] interview (e.g. Widgets Inc. interview)

LinkedIn search...
- [hiring manager name] (e.g. Lou Woodyard) Be sure to study their profile and their activity. Read any publications or posts that they have liked or commented on. That will help you understand what's important to them.
- [business name] (e.g. Widgets Inc.)

When you search the business on LinkedIn, under the *people* tab, type [job] to find current staff in the organization who are doing your job. For example, a marketer would type *home depot* and then within *home depot* they would search for *marketing* in the *people* category. Read their profiles. That will help you understand the people you might be working with, and how they fit into the workplace. Doing that will also make you show up in LinkedIn's *"people who recently looked at your profile"* area. A friendly photo and crafted headline might be enough to encourage an employer (and others) to checkout your (amazing) LinkedIn profile.

Has anyone in the business you're researching commented on or posted anything that should be reflected in either your employer or workplace avatars? Does the workplace have any products, services, processes, software tools, etc. that you don't know about. If so, you need to research them so that your job application has a better chance of aligning with the job's description. YouTube is often a good enough resource for this.

On the general avatars you created in part two, cross items out or add in new ones to reflect your job specific research. Now you're ready to work on your résumé and cover letter.

PRESENCE PYRAMID LEVEL 5: How to write a job application

Most people think that a job application should be focused on the person writing it. That it should mainly document previous employment, education, etc. On the contrary. Your application will be far more effective if you turn that idea on its head. You need to have your employer front and center of your mind.

Employers are people, just like you, but they experience the job market from a different perspective. You want a job. They want to fill a position. You're cursing at having to apply for lots of jobs and not getting interviews. They're cursing having to wade through a pile of sub-standard applications. Like you, employers have likes, dislikes, and feelings. And, mirroring life itself, what resonates with one employer may not resonate with another. There may be no silver bullet, but there is better engineered weaponry!

When they're reading your job application, employers don't want to know about you as a person. Until they get to the final stage of recruiting, they're unlikely to humanize you. They may as well be buying a new office machine. They just want to know how you can help them solve their problems. And they want you to provide evidence to support your claims.

Your application should be laser focused on a job's description, have a firm foundation in the research you did in part two, and be bolstered by the research you did on the employer's workplace.

Writing a job application is a mixture of art and science. There's two parts to it. Your résumé and your cover letter.

For some (mostly large) employers, your résumé will need to be formatted for two audiences. First to make it through Applicant Tracking Software (ATS) assessment, and then through human assessment.

It takes time to do a good job of writing a résumé. So, take a deep breath. Take a step back. Relax. Adopt a professional attitude. Good groundwork will pay dividends. It sends a message that, even if you're unemployed, you're taking the time to look for the right job. This subtle message gives employers greater confidence to hire you.

Résumé overview

Between the research you did for your LinkedIn profile and avatars, your networking, and your knowledge about yourself, you already have everything that need to write your résumé. Now you need to organize, format and make all that relevant to the job you're applying for.

A résumé is a marketing document that is customized to the job that you're applying for. It's different to a CV, which is a detailed history of academic achievements (and mostly used when applying for academic positions).

A résumé is not a place to be shy! If you don't demonstrate to an employer why you're well qualified for the job, then how are they meant to find out? It's not an employer's job to read between the lines. It's your job to make it obvious to them. That means none of this... *but I don't need to say that because it's a basic part of the job.* SAY IT! Ever heard of a concept called the *curse of knowledge?* That's when you know a topic so well that you can't imagine that anyone else could not know it too. Things that are second nature to you, are not necessarily so to other people. Michelle Robin says

> *With every bullet on your résumé, ask yourself, would someone ... [else] have an understanding of what I accomplished? If you're not sure, give your résumé to a friend and ask them to tell you what they believe you accomplished.*[58]

You also need to format your résumé in a way that captures your hiring manager's attention. Imagine you're reading a news site.

---

58 Michelle Robin, undated, The Curse of Knowledge: How it Affects Your Career and What to Do About It, https://ivyexec.com/career-advice/2018/curse-knowledge-impact-career

---

What is it about one article that captures your attention, but not another? The odds are that it's a crafted headline and teaser about something that interests you. That's what you résumé needs to be like. BAM! BAM! BAM! An employer wants your résumé to be easy to read and relevant to the job being filled.

Faced with hundreds of applications for a single job, your application will be skimmed and placed in a *yes*, *no*, or *maybe* pile. You need to make sure yours makes it into the yes pile. How do you do this? The key is to make your application easy to evaluate. It needs to...

- Be set out so that a quick glance will inspire an employer to read it in depth.
- Be customized to the hiring manager and workplace you're applying to, and easy to compare to the job description. That means that you need to use the same key words, and as much as possible, organize your responses to be in the same order as they appear in the job description. Some employers will have their job descriptions organized as checklists. Make it easy for them to check things off!
- Be targeted, concise, well organized, clear and free from spelling mistakes and grammatical errors.
- Demonstrate that you have standards, experience, skills, knowledge and qualifications.

How to format your résumé for Applicant Tracking Software (ATS)[59]

The main idea behind this book has been to show you how to avoid competing with a large group of applicants for a job. That's not always possible. Sometimes you'll apply for a job that's advertised online, and you'll come up against an ATS.

Let's consider two equally qualified candidates. Why does one of their résumé's make it through an ATS, and the other not?

---

59 **Further reading**
Paige Liwanag, February 25 2021, Don't Make These ATS Formatting Mistakes, https://www.jobscan.co/blog/ats-formatting-mistakes
Kristen M Fife, Nov 1 2020, BOTS in the ATS? Mostly a MYTH, https://www.linkedin.com/pulse/bots-ats-mostly-myth-kristen-fife-she-her-hers-/
Amy Miller, July 2020, WHY was my resume rejected?? Who's reading these anyway?: https://www.youtube.com/watch?v=3NQ6J-SJdsU

Sometimes that's about knowing how to write for an ATS. Here's an example of what I mean. Years ago, I sat an aptitude test to be trained as a software engineer. I failed miserably. Over the next week I read a *how to do aptitude tests* book. I re-sat the exam, and passed easily. My aptitude for writing software had not changed, but my ability to do aptitude tests had. And so it is for a résumé. You can be trained to write a résumé that passes through an ATS net, but that's only part of the puzzle. Your résumé still needs enough pizazz to gain you an interview.

Understanding what ATS are and how they're used can give you a leg-up in the job market. ATS need not be scary. They are just imposing a level of rigor onto your job application that should have been there in the first place.

ATS are a class of software in the same way that spreadsheets and word processors are. Each ATS is slightly different. Some are more advanced than others. All are constantly improving. Their job is to organize all the applications for a job, and to compare each applicant's résumé to the job's description. Most take your application, scan and Optical Character Recognition (OCR) it into text. They then reorganize it so that every applicant's résumé is formatted to be the same. That makes it easier for the recruiter to compare résumés to each other.

ATS are setup to look for words and terms that are in the job description and are specific to the role. Recruiters can search for these words. Some ATS highlight them in the recruiter's onscreen version of your résumé. In just a few seconds your résumé can move onto the next stage of the process if there's lots of highlighted words, compared to the *no* pile if your application only has a few highlighted words. In part one I suggested that employers often want a shortlist of around 10 or so applicants, and that there's different ways by which they can arrive at that those 10. The magic number of 10 highlights the importance of making sure your application gets prioritized within an ATS, especially because advertised jobs commonly have hundreds of applicants.

This is not rocket science. ATS, like all software are dumb. They can only work with what you give them. That means that you need to format your résumé so its easy for the ATS to read, reorganize, and then compare to the job description. As a general guide...

- **Use simple fonts:** Aerial or times roman are best. Preferably 10–12 pt. These are likely to OCR without error.
- **Don't use Tables:** The lines around tables confuse them.
- **Don't use fancy symbols and emoticons:** Fancy symbols and emoticons confuse them.
- **Keep headings simple:** Ideally, you should adopt the terminology used in the job description.
  – **No:** *Jobs I've Loved.*
  – **Yes:** *Work Experience*
- **Date formatting:** Dates should be month and year (MM/YYYY), not just year.
  – **No:** 2020-2021, 2020–21.
  – **Yes:** 01/2020–06/2021 or January 2020–June 2021.
- **Accidental spacing between words:** Check that you haven't accidently added extra spaces between words. Some ATS will see "software engineer" as one word, and "software   engineer" as two words. That means if you're applying for a job as a software engineer, an extra space between "software" and "engineer" will prevent some ATS from recognizing your qualification.
- **Left align your text:** Justified text might add spaces between important words (see the software engineer example above).
- **Automatic résumé rejection:** ATS usually only automatically reject résumés due to basic job requirements such as *"age 18+"* for bar jobs, or *"has driver's license"* for driving jobs.

Some people say that you should paste the job description into a word cloud generator such as wordclouds.com, and then make sure you use words that show as being important. Word clouds work for some job descriptions but not others. Often you only need to read the job description closely to work out which words are important (sometimes called keywords). Whatever you do, once you've identified important words, don't try and trick the ATS by using them so much that your résumé is nonsensical for a human to read. This is known as *keyword stuffing* and will lead to rejection by humans.

Once you've finished your application, compare it to the job description by pasting them both into the free online ATS at jobscan.co. Jobscan will analyze your application and provide you with guidance on how you can improve it so that its more ATS friendly. I show you how to use the free version of Jobscan in this section's video.[60]

Résumé design

There's two schools of thought on résumé design...

1. **Design school:** You need a well presented résumé so that you can attract an employer's attention. This is an idea that dates back to pre ATS times, and continues to be promoted by people who sell résumé templates. Margaret Magnarelli's blog post showing infographic résumé examples for graphic designer and marketer jobs is an example of this school of thought.[61]
2. **Anti design school:** Résumés with design elements in them do not make it through the first cut because they confuse Applicant Tracking Software.

Do not use a designer résumé template unless design is a core skillset for the job you're applying for, and you know that your résumé will not be fed into an ATS.

My call is that you should avoid designer résumés unless design is a core skillset for the job you're applying for, and you *know* that your résumé will not be fed into an ATS.

If you insist on going down the design path, call the hiring manager and ask them if they're okay with that. If nothing else, that's an excuse to make yourself known to them. Failing that, upload your

---

60 https://bit.ly/wsjsd-3-2
61 Margaret Magnarelli, undated, These are 8 of the most eye-catching resumes we've ever seen, https://www.monster.com/career-advice/article/best-infographic-resumes

designer résumé to LinkedIn and add an item called *Résumé Infographic* with a link to it in the contacts area of your ATS formatted résumé. Make sure your link is easy to read. Consider using a free URL shortener such as bitly, owly or tinyurl[62] to make your link memorable. For example *bit.ly/Alex-johnson-résumé-infographic.*

Think hard before you outsource a fancy résumé design. It can backfire. An employer might expect you to have design skills. Then again, they might also worry that you'll be more interested in designing stuff rather than doing your job.

Anatomy of a résumé

Many people unnecessarily agonize over résumé design. Its far more important to address the job description, quantify, and brand-align. I provide you with worked examples using a simple résumé format in part four.

As much as possible, organize your application to be in the same order and with the same wording as the items appear in the job description document.

Use bold letters to match key phrases in your résumé to key phrases from the job description. Two pages of 10–12 pt Times Roman or Arial font is about right.

- **Heading:** Your name and relevant qualification. Position ID and, as appropriate, email, phone, suburb, LinkedIn profile and relevant web details (e.g. website, Pinterest).

- **Executive summary:** In ~100 words, summarize your key skillsets as they relate to the job description. And how you have used your relevant skills to benefit a previous workplace. Think of this as the headline and leading paragraph of a news story. Faced with a screen full of executive summaries, would you click on yours?

- **Expertise:** Six or so dot points highlighting your key relevant skillsets.

- **Expertise demonstrated/work history:** For each position (volunteer, paid, relevant project, ...)

---

62 **Resources:** https://bitly.com, https://hootsuite.com/pages/owly, https://tinyurl.com

- Name of organization and dates (e.g. January 2020–June 2020 or 01/2020–06/2020)
  - Position
  - Short summary (~50 words)
  - Responsibilities in the role
- **Education:**
  - Place of study
  - Highlight good marks. No need to mention bad marks.
- **Additional skills:** Especially those relevant to the job. Often relevant school or university projects can be framed to be work experience.
- **Competency levels:** Be honest about your competency level on your résumé. I show you worked examples of this idea in part four.
- **Referees:** Available on request (see Q&A below).

Align yourself with brands and quantify your achievements

Your *presence* that I've been helping you build is a micro personal brand. In the *executive summary* and *expertise demonstrated* sections of your résumé, you can bolster this by aligning yourself with bigger brands. So, if you worked for a famous client, mention them by name (so long as that's not undermining client confidentiality).

You also need to "quantify". That means attaching numbers to achievements whenever you can. Google search: *[job] intern résumé quantification example*

This is not bragging, grand standing or self-promoting as some people would have you think. As I've said before, *how are people meant to find things out about you if you don't tell them?* Which of the following two examples do you think a hiring manager would be more likely to notice?

Example 1 (before brand alignment): 01/2020–06/2020. Accounting intern at ABC Co.

Example 2 (after brand alignment): 01/2020–06/2020. Accounting intern at ABC Co, corporate advisers to Google and Facebook.

Table 8 contains some worked examples of both brand alignment and quantification...

Table 8: Brand alignment and quantification examples.*

BASIC: Before brand alignment and quantification:	BETTER: After brand alignment	BEST: After brand alignment and quantification
Marketing: I was a marketing intern at JB Advertising where I assisted with an online marketing campaign.	I was a marketing intern at JB Advertising where I assisted with an online campaign for [some famous client].	I was a marketing intern at JB Advertising where I assisted with an online campaign for [some famous client]. My copyrighting was directly responsible for increasing clickthrough rates from 5% to 17%.
Content creator: Content creator at JB advertising where I created Facebook videos.	Content creator at JB advertising where I created Facebook videos for [some famous client].	Content creator at JB advertising. [Some famous client] consistently reported 8+% engagement rate for the Facebook videos I created for them. The industry standard is 6%.
Logistics: I was a logistics intern.	I was a logistics intern for [some famous transport company].	I was a logistics intern for [some famous transport company]. While there I developed a procedure that reduced process related returns from 5% to 2%, so saving $2m annually.
Volunteer: I was a volunteer.	I was a volunteer for [some famous charity].	As a volunteer for [some famous charity], a [city] based organization with 500 staff, supported by $50m in annual donations, and servicing 5000 clients each day, I supervised 4 administration interns.

BASIC: Before brand alignment and quantification:	BETTER: After brand alignment	BEST: After brand alignment and quantification
Administration: As an admin worker at JB Cabinets, I coordinated site fit outs.	As an admin worker at JB Cabinets, I coordinated site fit outs for the boardrooms of fortune 500 companies and national football clubs.	As an admin worker at JB Cabinets, I coordinated site fit outs for the boardrooms of fortune 500 companies and national football clubs. Fit outs often involved 20+ staff, transport and night work. They were often completed in a single night.
Barista: I was a barista.	I was head barista at [some famous café].	As head barista at [some famous café], I was in charge of 5 staff. I introduced procedures that made staff work more efficiently, and improved and standardized the customer experience. During the short time I was there, café turnover increased by 30%.

* Put yourself in an employer's boots. Which examples would be more likely to grab your attention?

Cover letter

As with every facet of recruiting, there's conflicting opinions about cover letters.[63] They are redundant for ATS assessment purposes, but useful for human assessment. My call is that because you can never be sure exactly how your job application will be treated, you should always include a cover letter.

Cover letters are where you make your résumé relevant to a job description. They're not a place to simply repeat what's in your résumé. They're where you go above and beyond what the job description is asking for. They're useful because you can send them in the body of an email, and as an attachment.

Anatomy of a Cover letter

- **Personal details:** email, phone, suburb (if appropriate), LinkedIn profile, position ID.
- **Addressed to a person:** Never "Dear Sir/Madam" or "To whom it may concern"

Look at the company website to find this out. If it's not there, call the company and ask.

"Hello. My name is Alex. I'm applying for the [job name] position. I'm just wondering who I should address my application to?"

The hiring manager might answer the phone, so be prepared for any questions you might get asked. Having had personal contact with them increases the likelihood that they will look out for your application. Making a good impression on the telephone might graduate you into the yes pile for interview, and a bad impression into the no pile!

How to send your job application to an employer

Unless specifically instructed otherwise, always send your application as both a pdf and a word document. Add your contact details and LinkedIn profile page to the footer of your email. Before they forward your application onto a prospective employer,

---

63 Isabel Thottam, undated, Is the cover letter finally dead? This will forever change how you apply for jobs. https://www.monster.com/career-advice/article/do-you-still-need-a-cover-letter

recruiters may convert it into their own format. To prevent unscrupulous employers from dealing with you directly, don't be surprised if a recruiter removes your contact details.

You're in luck if you did an informational interview with someone in the job's workplace. That's an opportunity to telephone them and ask for help. Without anyone realizing, your informational interview might have been a screening interview. Their recommendation, if they give it, will carry weight. Word of mouth recruiting is so important to some businesses that they offer a bonus to employees who refer recruits. So, making this call *before* you apply for the job may incentivize your contact to help you.

You could say something along the lines of...

Hi Sam. Its Alex here. You might recall that I interviewed you a while ago about [your job]. Thanks for that. Your feedback led me to close [XYZ] expertise gaps and helped give my résumé more focus. I'm about to apply for the [job title] at your workplace. I'd love to get an interview and I was wondering if you might be able to give me some insights into how your business' hiring process works.

They may just tell you how the process works, then advocate for you without your knowledge. They may also offer to help by making calls, sending emails, or even making a personal introduction. If they offer to help you, then you need to say something like. *Thanks so much for that Sam. Before you do anything, do you mind if I email you the application I was about to send off, and a link to my LinkedIn profile?* The idea behind that is to ensure that Lou has as much ammunition as possible to advocate on your behalf.

How to deal with rejection

Getting knock backs can be hard to take, but you need to expect these when you're job seeking. Self-esteem commentators will tell you that rejection *is not against you, it's for the other person.* It's important to understand that. It's okay to be sad, but you need to take the knock back and not dwell on it. Employers have been known to reject someone for an advertised job and then make contact days later with a different job offer. The positive that comes out of every rejection is that the preparation you do for every job application improves your chances for the next one. Everything about every level of your *presence pyramid* is improved.

Jenni Gritters and Wudan Yan from *the writers co-op* podcast never burn bridges. When someone rejects their pitch, they frame it that the timing and fit for the story is not right – they don't take it as a rejection. That way they can always pitch to that publication or editor again. It's a good attitude to have. It allows both of them to work on and off in places that have previously laid them off.

Bla bla bla. More advice! I'm sure you're sick-up-and-fed of hearing all the cliches from the generals behind the lines. The experience is different when you're in the trenches. Looking for work can be challenging, and so it's important to work on having a positive mindset.

Different people find that different things help them in challenging times. You need to find the thing that helps you. Friends, physical activity, relaxation exercises work for some. Avoid self-destructive crutches like excessive alcohol consumption or substance abuse. You need to be sharp and not sidelined by brain fog.

My secret is to listen to podcast episodes about people overcoming the odds – *How I built this*, *The Writers Co-op*, and *Conversations* on Australia's ABC are podcasts I often listen to. My twenty-something niece listens to *Seize The Yay*. My point is that some of you will find it useful to find two or three podcasts that resonate with you, lift you and inspire you. Listen to them regularly. Knowing that there's other people out there who have faced life challenges and overcame them can be hugely motivating.

Here's some examples of podcast episodes that I've found inspiring. Of the podcasts, the *how I built this* podcast is my favorite because Guy Raz consistently asks his guests about their life stories. After listening to a few episodes you start to understand that its common for people to spend time just fumbling through life before things fall into place for them. Google the titles to find them...

How I built this, MAY 3 2021: Eleven Madison Park: Daniel Humm[64]

Daniel dropped out of school at 14 to become a competitive cyclist. Later he became a teen dad and supported his family by being a kitchen hand. Daniel discovered he had a talent for food. Years later he runs Eleven Madison Park, a three Michelin star restaurant ranked as number one in the world.

How I built this, October 19 and October 26, 2020: McBride Sisters[65]

Robin and Andrea McBride have built one of the biggest black owned wine businesses in the world. It's an amazing story on many levels, especially seeing as neither sister knew the other existed until they were adults.

How I built this, July 19 2021, Bobbi Brown Cosmetics: Bobbi Brown (2018)[66]

This podcast is one of my favorites. Bobbi was never afraid to talk to people about what she did. She built her professional network while doing low paid jobs early in her career. That's what led her to higher paying jobs and later into business.

Jenni Gritters and Wudan Yan, March 23 2020, The writers co-op episode 3, Werk It[67]

Jenni and Wudan talk about how they use relationships to get work. Jenni and Wudan are successful jobbers, so their use of relationships and the importance they place on them is worth paying attention to.

Jenni Gritters and Wudan Yan, May 4 2020, The writers co-op episode 6, Building Relationships.[68]

This is the episode where Jenni and Wudan talk about networking and informational interviews. How they went about them when they were starting out, and how you should go about them.

64 https://www.npr.org/2021/04/28/991668793/eleven-madison-park-daniel-humm
65 https://www.npr.org/2020/10/15/924227706/mcbride-sisters-wine-part-1-of-2-robin-mcbride-and-andr-a-mcbride-john
https://www.npr.org/2020/10/23/927158151/mcbride-sisters-wine-part-2-of-2-robin-mcbride-and-andr-a-mcbride-john
66 https://www.npr.org/2021/07/16/1016898855/bobbi-brown-cosmetics-bobbi-brown-2018
67 https://www.thewriterscooppod.com/episodes/episode3
68 https://www.thewriterscooppod.com/episodes/buildingrelationships

ABC Australia conversations March 13, 2020: Building a school for the world's poorest children – Gemma Sisia's story[69]

Gemma and her 7 brothers were brought up on a 100,000 acre sheep property in the Australian Outback. Gema met her husband in Tanzania and decided to start a school there to educate local children for free. In 2019, year 12 students at her school ranked first in Tanzania for mathematics and in the top 10% nationally for all other subjects.

ABC Australia conversations February 11, 2021: Upside down in Bass Strait[70]

Will Oxley was crew on boat in the 1998 Sydney to Hobart yacht race. The boat with two crew on deck, capsized in 160 kmh (100 mph) winds. Both were attached by safety rope and found themselves back on deck when another wave hit and the boat righted it again. The rescue helicopter, on auto-hover at 76 metres (250 feet), abandoned its rescue when a wave broke over its skids. In the end, the battered boat limped back into port under its own power.

Seize the Yay, July 15 2021, Sarah Andrews // From spatial science and stormy seas to settling in Strahan at Captain's Rest

Sarah talks about growing up, the pressures to go to university so she could get a good job, and then having a great job but still not liking it. Finally, her journey to owning an Airbnb in Tasmania Australia.

Résumé FAQ

What should I say about my competency levels

Be honest about your competency levels. For example...

- **Expert:** Photoshop, MS-Office
- **Proficient:** email marketing, Facebook marketing
- **Novice:** Google analytics

---

69 https://www.abc.net.au/radio/programs/conversations/gemma-sisia-st-judes-tanzania/12035454

70 https://www.abc.net.au/radio/programs/conversations/will-oxley-sailing-sydney-to-hobart-celestial-navigation/13123728

Should I add an additional skills section?

Include additional skills if they are relevant to the job but are not in the job description. For example, a software engineering job description might call for knowledge of only one language. You would list other languages you know as additional skills.

Should I include a cover letter with my job application?

Yes. A cover letter is a place to elaborate on aspects of your résumé in a way that's relevant to a human assessor. The people who say you don't need one, mostly work in organizations that use applicant tracking software.

Is it okay to lie on my résumé?

No. While you can bask in the glory of having tricked someone into employing you, unless you quickly get up to speed, you risk being laid off during your probation period. Every industry has a community, and they talk! A wrong move with one employer can make it hard to get a job with another. Also, in some places a résumé is considered a legal document. Lying could open you up to legal proceedings.[71]

What if I had bad marks at college?

No need to mention bad marks.

What about referees?

Some people say referees are implied so there's no need to mention them. My call is to say *referees available on request*. That shows that you understand that referees are important and that you can provide them. It also demonstrates that you can be discreet and are not prepared to give people's details out willy-nilly.

Is there a difference between a résumé and a curriculum vitae (CV)?

Yes. There is a difference.

- **Résumé:** A résumé is a marketing document that is customized to the job that you're applying for. That means

---

71 Anna Kelsey-Sugg and Damien Carrick, 18/02/2022, Embellishing the truth in a CV is common. But here's where you can cross the line into fraud, https://www.abc.net. au/news/2022-02-18/how-cv-lies-can-become-a-criminal-offence/100809454

that it should be focused on the training and skillsets that are relevant to the job you're applying for. It also means that sometimes it's appropriate to leave things out.

- **Curriculum Vitae (CV):** A CV on the other hand translates from Latin to mean *"life's work"*. A CV therefore is a full account of everything that you've done and applies mostly to academic positions.

What if my degree is not relevant to the job I'm applying for?

If it's your only degree, you should include it in your résumé even if you think it's irrelevant. Fear not. There are some important things that a degree demonstrates to an employer. It shows an employer that you can start something and finish it, that you can research, write and think, and that you were good enough at all these things to be awarded a degree.

What education should I include on my résumé?

Include in-progress and completed degrees. Omit secondary school education where you have post-secondary education. If you have multiple qualifications only include the most relevant. Otherwise you risk being labelled as over qualified.

I'm overqualified for a job. How should I deal with that on my résumé?

Sometimes life circumstances make it necessary to apply for jobs that you're overqualified for. Overqualified candidates can be intimidating to employers, so you're right to be concerned about this. Assuming you've been asked to provide a résumé and not a CV (see definition above), then leaving off advanced qualifications is okay. But never lie on your résumé. Whether or not a résumé is a legal document is a gray area in law. Don't leave yourself open to legal proceedings.

What do you I say if I'm unemployed?

Don't lie. Put an end date on your last job and list your current position as *open to opportunities*. Covid has left many people unemployed. It's also common for graduates to take a gap year these days. Employers understand that. It's something to explain in an interview.

What if I was fired or I quit from my last job?

Leave this detail off your job application. It's something to address honestly and diplomatically in an interview.

At no stage in the recruitment process should you bag your previous employer. That behavior sets off alarm bells. If you're bagging your old workplace, what would you about your new workplace if you moved on?

There are plenty of good explanations for why you would leave a job. Far too many to list here. I suggest you google *What to say about a previous workplace that you resigned from* and find a reason that resonates with you.

As for being fired (as different from being *laid off*). That one requires some reflection on your behalf. You should make an effort to put your emotions aside and treat your situation as an opportunity for personal and professional growth. Google *what to say about a previous workplace that you were fired from*. There's a body of literature that will help you turn this negative into a positive. That may involve chatting to old colleagues, friends, and even your old job's HR department to try and unpack what went wrong.

You need to take the time to get on top of this. Not only because its possible you'll be asked about it in an interview situation, but also because you'll need to work on any personal characteristics that might lead to this happening again. Then again, it may just be that you're not suited to the sorts of jobs you've been fired from. For example, if you find that you're always getting fired for arguing with customers, then maybe you're not suited to jobs that involve customer service.

What do I say about an employment gap?

The good news that due to covid, employers have become used to seeing this on résumés. Employment gaps are common these days anyhow. Never lie about an employment gap. No tricky stuff like fudging it by just putting employment years down rather than months and years. It's much easier to check up on someone than it used to be, and if you're outed as a liar then an employer would be within their rights to overlook you on the basis that you're untrustworthy.

Add an item with dates in your employment section with a simple explanation such as *family leave, study leave, travelling, …*

I've been job hopping. How do I explain that?

Be honest. But emphasize the skills you gained by hopping and the outcomes for each of your employers. Maybe your jobs were fixed term contracts?

I'm strapped for time. Is it okay to send a job application from my current workplace?

NO. You should not send your application from your current employer's email or use their stationery. There are two parts to this…

1. **You're stealing time and stationery from your current employer:** Emails are time stamped so sending it during the day would means that you're stealing time from your current employer. Using their stationery mean that your stealing stationery.

2. **You're stealing brand from your current employer:** Using your employer's logo or domain name implies their endorsement.

Both send a subtle message that you're unprofessional, unable to be discreet, and that you'd treat your new employer the same way.

Should I include hobbies?

No. Not unless they relate to the job you're applying for.

Should I include a photo?

No. Employers can see a photo of you on LinkedIn if they need to. Also, photos can sometimes confuse applicant tracking software.

Should I include links to social media?

No. Not unless they are relevant to the job you're applying for. For example, creatives may link to Pinterest.

Should I include links to my website?

No. Not unless they its relevant to the job you're applying for. For example, journalists may link to their blog and web coders to a website they've built.

Is it OKAY to use buzzwords?

No! Can you think outside the box? Take the bull by its horns. Perhaps you're a go-getter or a team player? You'll have an uphill battle if you use terms like these in your résumé. Put yourself in a hiring manager's boots. How would you feel reading meaningless phrases like that all day?

How long should my résumé be?

Ideally two pages or less. This is a subtle test that employers set to see how well you can summarize and present complex information. Albert Einstein said that *if you can't explain it simply, then you don't understand it well enough.* Do not try to make your résumé fit by using a small font. Small fonts can be difficult for a human to read and can be hard for an ATS to scan and OCR. 10–12 point Arial or Times Roman fonts are best.

What if my relevant experience is buried among my work history?

Create two employment sections – *relevant work experience* and *other work experience.*

What's the big deal about keywords?

Keywords are words that employers use when they're searching for employees.

- **In LinkedIn:** Use LinkedIn predictive search functionality to find words that are being searched for. Type a word in the search bar. If LinkedIn doesn't automatically suggest it, try using a different but related word.

- **In your job application:** The best keywords are ones that are within the job description, and often also words that are highly relevant to the job. To help you work out which keywords are important, use the predictive search functionality in google and LinkedIn, and of course, by carefully evaluating your job description.

- For a civil engineering job in the water industry, keywords might be things like *water pipe, asset, CAD, renewal, etc.*
- For a digital marketing job, keywords might be things like *social media marketing, email marketing, loyalty program, data analysis, etc.*

My thoughts on interviews

I don't want to talk in depth about interviews because, frankly of the many jobs I've ever had I've only ever attended two interviews. Both times I lucked it. Other than those, I've always got jobs by chatting to someone I already knew. Early in my working life I worked for family friends, and they introduced me to employers, and later I got work through people I met at conferences, through lecturers at university, or by teaming up with other consultants who had contacts.

As a small business owner, I never formally advertised a job or interviewed anyone. I always hired people via recommendations from colleagues or contacts at my old university.

My thoughts on wage negotiations

If someone told you that you could make thousands of dollars in one day, would you pay attention? Then read on.

When it comes to wage talks, be sure to know your worth. Through your informational interviews, you should have an idea of the business's experience with entry-level employees. Are they a bother to train? Are you likely to be more valuable to them? What is the wage range for entry-level employees in comparable workplaces? If it's $40,000–$50,000 a year, where do you think you should sit on that scale? Realistically I mean. Why do you think that? Be comfortable with what your worth is and why before you get into a situation where you might get caught off guard.

Lou: *So, what wage are you expecting?*

Alex: *Well, I've done some research and it seems that entry level range is $40,000, typically for people who have unrelated degrees, through to $50,000 for people who have highly relevant degrees.*

To be honest, I think I'm worth $50,000 because my course is relevant, it's from a university that is renowned for the quality of its graduates, and I'm trained in all the software's and processes that you use. That means that I'll require minimal on boarding. And I'm an active contributor to the [some relevant group] on LinkedIn, meaning that I have networks that have the potential to be useful to you.

Like many things in life, value is created at the beginning of the arrangement. Starting a job at your correct worth sets you up for better pay throughout your career. A 10% pay rise from $40,000 versus a 10% pay rise from $50,000 means that your first pay rise is $55,000 rather than $44,000.

If you can justify a better starting wage, know that it means less than you think to your employer.

If you can justify a better starting wage, know that it means less than you think to your employer. It becomes less important to them when you consider the on-costs of employing you – car, office space, government fees, insurances, etc. If you're a really good candidate who requires minimal supervision, and can become productive quickly, then they'll consider the extra money well spent. *Quality lasts long after price is forgotten* goes the old saying.

PART FOUR – Examples of job applications

Read this and then skip to the example that's relevant to you.

Entry level positions may be advertised, but often they're not. That's why I wrote about networking and informational interviews in part two. Sometimes networking is enough on its own to secure you a job. I did not apply for my research position when I was a new graduate. And I did not apply for my university teaching position. I did not apply for the job I was offered in my local State Mapping Agency. Without realizing, in each case, I was being tested out on smaller jobs before employers were comfortable offering me bigger jobs. I did not have to apply. I did not have to provide a résumé.

That said, I was naïve. Knowing what I know now and with the tools that are available now, I would have gone about things much differently. As you can imagine, I would have focused on creating my *presence pyramid* (even though it would have been difficult without the web and LinkedIn). Then I would have set out to find a job and employer combination that would have made me want to get out of bed in the morning.

In the absence of an ad for a job, sometimes an advertised job that's above your grade is a clue that a business is building capacity, and so should be a target for an informational interview. As a quick recap of what I showed you in part 2, here's an example of how, if you were a graduate in marketing, you would go about getting an informational interview...

- **Narrow down your field of marketing:** There are many types of jobs for marketers (e.g. digital marketing, market research, public relations, copywriting, branding, ...). Let's say *digital marketing*.

- **Choose a sector:** Choose from sectors like hospitality, health, retail, entertainment, and more. Let's imagine *retail*.

- **Possible workplaces:** Using the following google queries, look for news articles about growing retail businesses. You're best to limit the results to the last year or less (tools -> time -> past year)...

- **To find small listed companies (typically low hundreds of employees):**
  small caps "retail" in [your country / city]
  e.g. *small caps "retail" in New York.*
- **To find fast growing retailers:**
  fastest growing retail companies in [your country / city]
  e.g. *fastest growing retail companies in America*

From the google results, choose a subsector that aligns with your interests and values. For a google search of *fastest growing retail companies in America* there were a gazillion results about small cap listed companies. After reading a few blog posts I decided to delve deeper into the following two examples...

- Sonic Automotive (NYSE code is SAH): Automotive retailer
- Citi Trends, Inc. (NYSE code is CTRN): Fashion retailer.

Find the latest annual report for a small cap: google *[company name] annual report* OR *[company name] investor presentation.* Both Sonic Automotive and Citi Trends have annual reports that suggest they're growing. I can say this because both report that they have increased earnings, and that they're adding new stores and systems. Growing companies are more likely to be hiring than matured companies. For someone looking for a graduate marketing job, the reports tell them the following...

- How the organization uses marketers. Using Sonic Automotive and Citi Trends as examples, when reading these reports, you should take note of the following points and ask yourself whether they represent opportunities for you. Are there things in these reports that you'd like to have the opportunity to learn, or perhaps there are skills you have that you think might help them lift their game...
  - The sophistication (or lack of) of the analyses in the investor presentations.
  - Strategic placement of stores, demographic analysis of customers, focus on branding.
- >100 marketing staff in each business (LinkedIn search)

Having done this level of research, you should be in a position to create avatars for both your hiring manager and workplace, quickly fill gaps in your skillset and reflect your alignment with the job in your LinkedIn profile, résumé and cover letter.

With the recap out of the way, assuming you've done the research I talked about in part two, your *presence* should make you a good choice for the job you're applying for. There's four things I want you to notice about the job application examples that follow...

1. The cover letter is a copy-paste-modified version of the LinkedIn *about* section.

2. The tone of my cover letters is friendly and conversational. They also tell a story. My cover letters contrast to the more formal style of cover letter that you often see around the web and in résumé writing literature. Read the cover letters for the example job applications that follow this. Then look at some more formal examples on the web (google [job] cover letter). Although my preference is for *friendly and conversational*, you need to decide which style is for you, and then make the cover letter your own.

3. My cover letter and résumé always link back to the job description and hiring manager and workplace avatars.

4. For each job, in each parallel universe, Alex does sometimes paid work, and sometimes unpaid work in small workplaces. Small workplaces often have a low barrier to entry and can offer a broader workplace experience than can't be had in internships with large organizations. Alex' focus in these positions is to build work experience that is directly relevant to the industry avatars created in part 2.

   Alex incorporates special projects into college coursework and presents results at a local business networking breakfast. Networking groups and even Rotary clubs are often on the lookout for guest speakers. Speaking to an audience is great social proof of Alex' professional worth.

I'm not going to provide worked examples of job applications for either Sonic Automotive or Citi Trends. Copyright laws prevent me from using their job advertisements. Instead, I've constructed the following three examples to be typical of job advertisements that you're likely to come across.

Notes on using photos of your Avatar

Yep. Using a photo of your actual hiring manager for your avatar sounds a little creepy. Casual observers could be forgiven for calling you out on that one. Here's my advice. Find a photo of your hiring manager if you can. Or at least someone you imagine looks like them. Print it out and have it in front of you while you create their avatar, and while you write your job application. The thing is that writing to someone makes your writing more personable. Then, when you've finished your job application, destroy the photo. I don't want anyone to think you're creepy! And I don't want to be accused of teaching you how to be creepy.

I have a confession to make. I was struggling to write the first draft of this book. Then one day I took my own advice. I found photos of two likeable college graduates, called them Miranda and Joel, printed them out and sat them on my desk while I was writing. Amazing. My writers block disappeared. My sub conscious didn't want to let them down.

As an exercise, write a short letter to someone you care about. Spend five or ten minutes writing without their photo in front of you, and then five or ten minutes writing to them with their photo directly in front of you. If you're anything like me, your writing style will change to be more personable and words will come easier to you.

Please leave a review

Now I have a favor to ask of you. It would mean a lot to me if you left a short, honest review for *The Job Hunting Book* on Amazon, Goodreads, or whatever online platform you prefer. I love seeing what my readers think of my work and how it has helped them (or, in the case of negative reviews, receiving constructive criticism that I can use to improve as a writer). Thank you. Ian

Goodreads link

Job application example 1: PARALLEL UNIVERSE #4 – Marketing Graduate

In this example Alex uses the family pizza shop as a vehicle to gain marketing experience. Not everyone has a family business that they can tap into, but plenty of businesses will let you help them. You're unproven and you need to gain experience, so pitch yourself as a marketing student who wants some practical marketing experience, will work for free, but requires a small marketing budget. Be sure to pick a business that has the potential to yield measurable results in a timeframe that's acceptable to you. You're offering to do valuable work for free, so you're wasting you're time unless you are sure that management...

- Have a marketing mindset.
- Will engage in the process.
- Will disclose measurables to you (e.g. #coupons presented, increased orders, etc.).

I suggest that you begin by producing a simple plan with one marketing channel in it (letter drops, google ads, Facebook ads, etc.). For each stage set out what you want to achieve, measure, and the budget you require. If you and the business can't agree on a small, well defined project scope (ideally in writing), then take your marketing plan, modify it, and present it to other businesses until you get a taker.

Who knows, if you get a good result, the business might employ you to widen the scope of the project to include other marketing channels. Maybe it could even be the beginnings of a side hustle for you?

THE AD – WANTED: Graduate Digital marketer

ABC-co is a local Thai street food Quick Service Restaurant making it big. In the last three years we have grown from four locations to eleven, and are on track to open ten new stores in the next 12 months. We're building a reputation for fast, fresh and flavorsome. We're obsessed with sharing our style of street food with the world.

The position

We value diverse, professional people who thrive in a dynamic environment that has a focus on continual learning, live ABC-co's values, and of course, you must love street food. Currently 15% of our sales are via digital channels. We want to make full use of our kitchens to double the value of that in the next 12 months and triple it the year after. The key driver of that will be improvements in our marketing, online, and instore systems.

We are looking for a recent graduate to join our digital marketing team. You will be part of a team that is responsible for building and maintaining our social media, website, loyalty program, e-commerce, email marketing, social media advertising, audience analysis, search engine optimization, search engine marketing, and ROI analyses of our Digital Marketing effectiveness.

Your new colleagues will train and nurture you, but you will be expected to grow professionally by working hard, smart and learn fast.

Key competencies

- Quick-service restaurant (or hospitality) experience highly regarded.
- Degree (or near completion) in marketing or similar.
- Confident to bring marketing ideas to the table.
- Able to turn data into insights.
- Proficiency in the Microsoft Office Suite (Word, Excel, PowerPoint).
- Thirst for knowledge and problem solving.
- Positive attitude and willingness to occasionally go above and beyond your job description with tasks that might be big or small.
- Exposure to...
  - Website maintenance.
  - Social media marketing.
  - Content marketing.
  - Email marketing.
  - Google Analytics.
  - Social media Analytics.

Benefits

- Start at minimum wage. Market-based performance review at end of 3 month probation. Annually after that.
- Free Street Eats Thursdays.
- We want you to be the best you can be as much as we want to be the best that we can be.
  - Continuous on the job training and professional development.
  - Following probation period, attend approved industry events on us.
- 20 days annual leave.
- 10 days sick leave.
- Public holidays.
- Birthday holiday.
- Family-friendly flexible work hours by arrangement.
- 401 k/pension/superannuation benefits.

Avatar for Alex's marketing hiring manager

Table 9: Marketing hiring manager avatar. See numbers in Figure 5.

HEADING	Your hiring manager – suggestions for answers
OVERVIEW (1)	
Photo of Lou or someone who looks like Lou.	Photo of Lou. Or a stock photo (e.g. pxhere.com, freeimages.com, commons.wikimedia.org). Only use famous people if that's who you're aspiring to work for.
Name	Lou Woodyard.
Age	Mid 30s
Job title	Manager of digital marketing
Personality traits	Affiliate [personality trait from Table 5]
Income	$100k
Reports to	CEO
Education	Bachelor of digital marketing from [institution].
Count of staff	Team of 5 people.
PERFORMANCE MEASURES (2)	
Performance measures	# satisfied clients, # improved services, # improved processes, workplace morale, business growth
BIO (3)	
Bio	Lou grew up in a family run Quick Service Restaurant (QSR) and loves the idea of being part of ABC-Co's success story.
QUOTE (4)	
Quote	I love being part of a QSR success story.
MOTIVATIONS (5)	
Money	**Profit:** Business growth
Values: What is important to them? What drives the decisions they make?	**Teamwork:** Build a happy and cohesive team. **Ideology:** Family history of struggling QSR and wants to be a part of a QSR success story.
ROLE AND RESPONSIBILITY (6)	
Overseeing implementations (10%)	Ensuring campaigns are rolled out in a manner that front line staff can manage.

HEADING	Your hiring manager – suggestions for answers
Writing specifications (15%)	Designing marketing campaigns.
Meetings (15%)	Meetings to discuss all aspects of the business. Including board meetings
Monitoring (10%)	Reviewing and approving campaigns prior to implementation.
Geography (10%)	Responsible for the entire geographical extent of ABC-Co's business
Return on Investment – ROI (40%)	Ensuring marketing efforts translate into business rewards.
GOALS (7)	
Expand business	Improve the customer experience (e.g. via ordering app). Open new restaurants. Introduce food trucks.
Staff supervision	Step back from day-to-day micro-management issues. Less staff supervision & increased focus on strategy.
Streamline business	Streamline production operations. Tame business data, especially analytics.
FRUSTRATIONS (8)	
Systems: Processes too complicated & stressful.	Too much time spent on micro-managing projects. There must be a better way.
Systems: Data overload	Masses of data, but no tools to easily manage and summarize it.
Systems: Lack of expertise	Already overworked. No time to learn and implement new systems
Constraints	Limited IT support. Narrow skillset of staff
INFLUENCES (9)	
Influences	Competitors, blogs, colleagues, entrepreneur influencers (Gary Vaynerchuck, Seth Godin, Jeff Walker)
SOFTWARE (10)	
Office suite, CRM, ...	Microsoft Office Marketing software (MailChimp, Hootsuite)

Avatar for the workplace Alex's marketing job is within

Table 10: Marketing workplace avatar. See numbers in Figure 6.

HEADING	The business – suggestions for answers
OVERVIEW (1)	
Photo: You need to be able to visualize your avatar. Find a photo that represents a widget they sell, or service they provide.	ABC-CO
Name: Business name	ABC-Co
Time in business	5 years
Employees	35 office staff, 200 full/part time restaurant staff
Income	$35m annual revenue
PERFORMANCE MEASURES (2)	
Performance measures	Annual growth >15% Raving customers
BIO (3)	
Bio	ABC-co is a fast growing Thai street food QSR. Three years ago we were 4 restaurants, now we're 11, and next year we'll be 21. On the back of our obsession with sharing our style of street food with the world, we're building a reputation for fast, fresh and flavorsome.
QUOTE (4)	
Quote	Growth on the back of fast, fresh and flavorsome.
MOTIVATIONS (5)	
Money	**Profit:** Sell more, grow.
Values: What is important to them? What drives the decisions they make?	**Ideology:** Ensure adherence to company standards **Teamwork:** Build a happy and cohesive team **Quality:** Focus on fresh ingredients
Clients (6)	
Clients	Typical clients are in their 20s to mid 30s time poor career builders who value fast, fresh and flavorsome.

THE JOB HUNTING BOOK © 2022 IAN ALLAN

HEADING	The business – suggestions for answers
Client pain points and frustrations	Delay b/w order and delivery too great Not available in enough locations
Geography	Eastern metro.
GOALS (7)	
Systems	New project management systems New office systems New customer engagement systems New supply chain systems
FRUSTRATIONS (8)	
Hard to find qualified staff	Recruiting restaurant staff is time consuming and extra work
Staff availability is unreliable	Too much time wasted reorganizing restaurant shifts
Systems: Office	Need better coordination between teams
Systems: Current processes complicated and stressful.	Too much time spent on managing projects.
Systems: Data overload	Masses of data, but no tools to easily manage and summarize it.
Systems: Lack of expertise	We're rolling out new systems and software, but nobody knows how to use them.
Productivity	Lots of work being done, but too little of it is productive.
Constraints	Limited IT support. Narrow skillset of staff.
EMPLOYEE BENEFITS (9)	
	20 days annual leave, Public holidays, 10 days sick leave, Pension fund, Flexible hours, Work at home or office.
SOFTWARE (10)	
Office suite, CRM, ...	Microsoft Office Xero accounting Marketing software (MailChimp, Hootsuite) Monday

Figure 5: The Digital Marketer avatar graphic. See numbers in Table 9

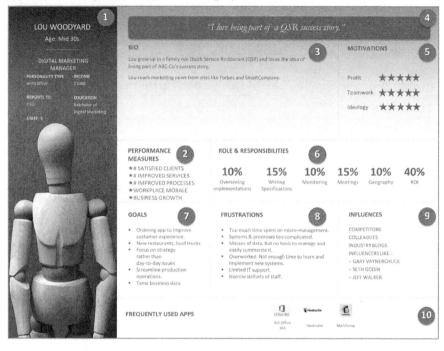

Figure 6: The Quick Service Restaurant avatar graphic. See numbers in Table 10

Alex's LinkedIn Profile: It has a digital marketing focus

The information below is discussed in detail in the LinkedIn section. The capitalized letters relate to those in Figure 4.

Contact information (A)

- Profile Name: alex-johnson-digital-marketer
- Email: alex-johnson-digital-marketer@somedomain.com
- Website: samspizza.com

Job preferences (B)

- Check the box to say that you're looking for work.

Intro section (C)

- Basic information: Fill in obvious things like name, location, industry, education.
- Headline: Digital marketer seeking graduate position
- Photo: Friendly and consistent with other ABC-Co office staff you find on LinkedIn.

About (D)

Hi. I'm Alex

I have a confession. I'm obsessed with brand personality and the perfect online customer experience. I like rags to riches growth stories like Pip Snacks, Famous Dave's and McBride sisters.

I am a student of brands and successful QSRs like Pals Sudden Service. As brand and digital marketing manager in my family's Quick Service Restaurant, I've seen how effective digital marketing and branding can be. In the 18 months following my appointment, Sam's pizza's home delivery orders doubled. My focus on "phygital" – improved ecommerce experience, consistent look between drivers uniforms, packaging, and even handwritten on-package notes from chef to customer, led to a loyal, growing base of repeat customers. Of note, we gained prestigious clients and events such as...

- F1 Team socials.
- Regular fortune 500 consulting firm Friday socials.

- Patronage by personalities from nearby TV station that have resulted in occasional on-air plugs.

This business growth was fueled by the loyalty program I built using MailChimp and sweepwidget, moving the existing wordpress site and online ordering to shopify, improved training, and improved systems – ordering, pizza production (including kitchen layout), and delivery.

I think websites can be too complicated. That can lead to confusion for the customer and there's more to go wrong. The focus of my redesign of Sams' Pizza website was to stay simple, reinforce brand, and earn customer loyalty.

Featured content (E)

- Interesting blog posts that Alex read about digital marketing.
- Links to brands that resonate: Pal's sudden service, Siete Family Foods, Famous Daves, McBride Sisters and Chipotle.

PowerPoint presentations with voiceover commentary.

- What I did to make Sams Pizza such a success.
- College presentations about digital marketing.

Work experience (G)

Sam's Pizza. [March 2020] – present (part time). Brand and digital marketing manager. Won catering for...

- F1 Team drinks
- Regular fortune 500 consulting firm Friday socials.
- Local TV station socials.

Built a mailing list with 900 signups using MailChimp and sweepwidget. My squeeze page has a 12% conversion rate.

Migrated wordpress website to shopify and streamlined its online ordering. This led to a 30% decrease in cart abandonment compared to the previous website.

Increased online orders by 100%.

Implemented 45 minute home delivery guarantee by improving workplace systems and product standards, and then marketing heavily with hyperlocal Facebook ads and letter drops to increase penetration into a smaller delivery area.

Education (H)

Bachelor's degree in digital marketing at [some local college]. I used Sam's Pizza for my class projects. My favorite part of the course was list building and email marketing. At 12%, my email opt-in had the highest conversion rate in my class.

Skills, endorsements and recommendations (I & J)

Add skills such as Digital Marketing, email marketing, brand management and software.

Alex presented Sam's Pizza as an email marketing example at a local business networking breakfast (see accomplishments section), and asked attendees for endorsements and recommendations. Alex also asked for endorsements from a lecturer and as colleague from Sam's pizza.

Accomplishments (K)

Feature presenter on email marketing at a local business networking breakfast.

Interests (L)

Alex follows digital marketing influencers like Ryan Deiss, Gary Vaynerchuck.

Alex is a member of the *digital marketing*, and *email marketing gurus* groups.

Alex's Cover letter: Digital Marketer

Position number: 1234
Date: MM/DD/YYYY
Alex Johnson
E: alex.johnson@somedomain.com
T: 0123456789
L: linkedin.com/in/alex-johnson-digital-marketer
A: [your suburb]

Lou Woodyard
ABC-Co
ABC-Co address

Dear Lou

Thank you for your invitation to apply for the graduate marketing position at ABC-Co. I am a recent graduate in digital marketing from [college name].

I was born into a QSR family. I grew up talking about my family's pizza restaurant at the breakfast table. Managing staff, quality of ingredients, negotiating with suppliers, customer satisfaction and business building are all familiar topics. My experiences continued into adulthood, and I am proud to say that I am accomplished in every facet of the business.

I was always troubled that my parents seemed to work so hard, but never quite made it beyond their good reputation among some loyal locals. That led me to study marketing at college. There I became obsessed with brand personality and the perfect online customer experience.

When appointed as the Sam's Pizza digital marketing and brand manager, I became a student of brands. I took my learnings into the family business. Eighteen months on and the delivery side of the business has doubled. Much of that success is owed to my focus on "phygital" – phone answering standards, improved ecommerce experience, the consistent look between driver's uniforms and packaging, and even handwritten on-package notes from chef to customer.

I redesigned and moved the shop website to Shopify, ran competitions and linked them to a loyalty program powered by MailChimp. To support the "45 minutes or its free" guarantee, I improved the shops systems – pizza production (including kitchen layout) and delivery. The result was a bigger base of repeat customers. We also gained prestigious clients such as...

- Team socials.
- Regular fortune 500 consulting firm Friday socials.
- Patronage by personalities from a nearby TV station that have resulted in occasional on-air plugs.

Heading up the changes that transformed my family's business from a source of family wages into a genuine success story is the most satisfying thing I've ever done. Recently I began training an intern from [college name] to continue with the systems I built when I move on.

I sense that many of the things I have learned in building my family's QSR are relevant to ABC-Co's marketing needs. The satisfaction I felt watching my family's QSR grow in response to my marketing efforts was second to none. I would dearly love to play a role in ABC-Co's growth and perhaps experience that level of satisfaction again.

Thank you for your time and consideration. I look forward to meeting with you to discuss your exciting position in person.

Sincerely,

Alex Johnson

E:	Alex.Johnson@somedomain.com
T:	0123456789
L:	linkedin.com/in/alex-johnson-digital-marketer
Encl:	Alex-Johnson-Graduate-Digital-Marketer-Resume.docx
	Alex-Johnson-Graduate-Digital-Marketer-Resume.pdf

Alex's résumé: Digital Marketer

Alex Johnson,
Digital Marketer

E: alex.johnson@somedomain.com
T: 0123456789
L: linkedin.com/in/alex-johnson-
digital-marketer
A: [suburb]

EXECUTIVE SUMMARY

I am a digital marketer. Although I'm a recent graduate, I already have some successes. I have been brand and digital marketing manager in my family's Pizza Restaurant since March 2019. In that time, home delivery sales have doubled. I was able to work professionally and constructively with the full range of personalities and skillsets in the business to roll out some challenging changes in kitchen systems and layout, as well as delivery to customers. These were in support of my digital marketing and traditional marketing efforts that included Facebook ads, letter drops, list building and loyalty programs. A busy pizza kitchen taught me how to remain calm and level-headed under the pressure of deadlines. The final year of my degree was delivered remotely, demonstrating that I am able to work unsupervised.

EXPERTISE

- **Brand building**
- **Hands on QSR experience**
- **Facebook ads and analytics**
- **Project Planning and Estimating**
- **Stakeholder Management**
- **Project Reporting**

WORK HISTORY

Sam's Pizza   March 2020 – September 2021 (part time)

Sam's Pizza is a 70 seat Quick Service Restaurant. It has 3 fulltime restaurant staff, 12 part time restaurant and delivery staff, and 1.8 full time equivalent support staff. During this time the delivery business doubled, and attracted regular corporate clients.

Brand and Digital Marketing Manager

Successfully managed the full range of relationships involved in doubling the size of the home delivery side of the business. Focus on "phygital" (digital to physical customer experience).

- **Branding:** Coordinated and sourced uniforms and packaging to present a consistent look to customers. Developed scripts for pizza chefs to write personal notes on pizza boxes. Managed in support of my 45 minute delivery guarantee.

- **Facebook marketing:** Using staff knowledge of customers I developed a demographically and geographically focused Facebook ads campaign. One of my three offers performed significantly better. The campaign was cost neutral, but resulted in a bigger base of regular customers.

- **List building:** Built a list of 900 people with our weekly free pizza party competition. Tools were sweepwidget, Facebook and MailChimp.

- **Letter drops:** Designed pamphlets with different offers and delivered them in small areas to test them. Rolled out the best test campaign for an 8% increase on sales compared to previous weeks.

- **Stakeholder Management:** As the delivery business grew, the kitchen needed to increase output. I collaborated with kitchen staff to develop more efficient prep procedures, and redesigned the kitchen workstations to support this.

Sam's Pizza	November 2015 – March 2019 (part time)

Sam's Pizza is a 70 seat Quick Service Restaurant. It had 3 fulltime restaurant staff, 7 part time restaurant and delivery staff, and 1 full time support staff.

Pizza chef and deliveries

I trained as a pizza chef and assisted with deliveries.

- Monitoring of wood fired pizza oven.
- Preparation of pizza dough.
- Pizza prep and cooking.
- Inventory management and supply ordering

EDUCATION AND QUALIFICATIONS

Bachelor of Digital Marketing [college name]
March 2019 – November 2021

SKILLS

- Email marketing.
- Social media marketing (including targeting and analytics).
- Letter drop marketing.
- List building.
- Loyalty programs.
- Software:
  - **Intermediate:** Sweepwidget, MailChimp, Facebook ads and analytics.
  - **Advanced:** Word, Excel, PowerPoint,

ADDITIONAL SKILLS

- Feature presenter on email marketing at local business networking breakfast.

REFERENCES

Supplied on request.

Job application example 2: PARALLEL UNIVERSE #5 – IT Support Engineer

There are many paths to an IT career. And there are many versions of IT careers to be had. Level 1 support is a common entry point. Expectations will be low initially. You'll provide simple solutions to what will seem to be simple problems to you. You'll direct problems that you can't solve to more senior support staff. For Internet Service Providers (ISPs) you'll learn the server side of things. For Software As Service (SAS) businesses you'll learn about the application you're supporting and the business' clients.

I've picked the Moodle Learning Management System (LMS) as an example of a SAS support job. Moodle is the world's most used LMS. Online learning is a growth sector, so it's an example of a job you could realistically be on the lookout for. There are opportunities to build your basic skillset as a volunteer. Careers in support, system setup, sales, user experience, and development all come to mind.

Alex has found a small not for profit that uses the Moodle Learning Management System and volunteered with them. It's often easy to get appointed to a volunteer position with a small organization and the opportunities for gaining experience and collecting references and endorsements is great.

To find not for profits to volunteer with, Alex googled...

- *moodle site:.org.[country code]* e.g. *moodle site:.org.uk*
- *moodle [country] site:.org* e.g. *moodle america site:.org*

You'll also notice that Alex has teaching experience. When approached along the lines of... *I would like to get some teaching experience. Can I help you teach the Introduction to LMS section of IT 101?*, some professors will be open to letting you teach. You can only ask!

THE AD – WANTED: IT Support Engineer (Level 1)

Moodle-4-K-12 is a market leading provider of Moodle LMS solutions for mid size K-12 schools. Our clients are just big enough to need an LMS, but too small to employ their own LMS workforce. We distribute and support Moodle coupled with our own Moodle teaching solution. We support teachers so they can get on with teaching and so their students can get on with learning.

Moodle-4-K-12 is growing and as a result we are looking for an **IT Support Engineer (Level 1).** This is the perfect gateway to starting your IT career.

The diverse range of business roles in Moodle-4-K-12 (educators, developers and system setup and support) hints at the range of career opportunities that we offer. We encourage (and support) our people to identify what motivates them so they can write their own story, leveraging their interests and passions to be the best they can be. The career possibilities are endless. In fact, most of our senior team kick started their career with us as an IT support engineer and we now only promote from within.

The position

An exciting opportunity exists for an enthusiastic IT graduate (or equivalent) to join our Moodle-4-K-12 team. This is an entry-level role so we don't expect you to already be at the top of your game. Attitude, passion and eagerness to learn are key.

You will provide Tier 1 support for our Moodle installations. You will interact with customers and with our internal teams to solve problems. Your role includes...

- First-level help desk support to clients to troubleshoot and resolve configuration and operation issues with Moodle-4-K-12 via phone, email, and chat channels.
- Log, maintain, and complete IT support tickets using Zendesk.
- Ensure all incoming tickets are dealt with in the specified guidelines of our Service Level Agreements (SLA's), captured, resolved or referred to the correct person for action.

- Investigate issues and provide feedback to customers and colleagues as appropriate.
- Create and maintain user and technical documentation as instructed.
- Report on the need for system improvements and internal process improvements.
- Assist with the user testing of system modifications as required.
- Monitor to ensure client installations are operational within SLA uptime parameters.
- Site backups and restores.
- Email setup.

Key competencies

We're a collaborative team so you will like working with others and won't be afraid to share your ideas, ask questions or chat with colleagues and customers about the work you're doing. Most importantly, you're passionate about learning and have an insatiable hunger for exploring and understanding new ways of doing things.

The ideal candidate will have:

- Demonstrated understanding of a Learning Management System (preferably Moodle).
- IT support ticketing system experience (preferably Zendesk).
- Advanced communication skills (written, verbal and interpersonal) with the ability to cultivate relationships at all levels.
- Familiarity with PHP, JavaScript, HTML5, SQL and HTTP.
- Problem solving skills.
- Ability to follow documented procedures, prioritise tasks, and self-manage workload.
- Ability to work independently and in a team.
- Demonstrated experience working within a customer service focused role (even hospitality) with a demonstrated stable employment history.

- You will have completed (or nearly completed) relevant formal studies in Information Technology, or you will have relevant experience.
- Commitment to learning, taking direction and continuous improvement.

Benefits

We offer a supportive work environment that fosters individual responsibility and initiative. We also offer flexible working hours, and opportunities for our team to grow and expand their skill sets, including training, conference attendance and mentoring. Our fun and inclusive culture ensures that everyone enjoys coming to work each day.

- Competitive salary.
- 401 k / pension / superannuation benefits.
- Opportunities for career progression.
- Free onsite gym, personal trainers and group fitness sessions.
- Employee Assistance Program including access to a range of medical and counselling services.
- Free social functions.
- Interesting and challenging work that will stretch you.
- Opportunity to progress to other areas of the business, including LMS setup, sales and development.
- Further education/training opportunities.
- A collaborative and friendly team environment in a values-driven culture. We are open to change and are nimble.
- Initially office based with the possibility to become mostly home based after a 3 month probation period.

If you have a passion for LMS and feel you'd like to work with us, then send us a cover letter and résumé that demonstrate your experience and telling us why we need you! You should include links to any publicly available examples of relevant work.

Please provide the contact details for two referees.

Avatar for Alex's IT hiring manager

Table 11: IT hiring manager avatar. See numbers in Figure 7.

HEADING	Your hiring manager – suggestions for answers
OVERVIEW (1)	
Photo of Lou or someone who looks like Lou.	Photo of Lou. Or a stock photo (e.g. pxhere.com, freeimages.com, commons.wikimedia.org). Only use famous people if that's who you're aspiring to work for.
Name of the hiring manager.	Lou Woodyard
Age	Mid 30s
Job title	Manager of LMS support
Personality traits	Affiliate [personality trait from Table 5]
Income	$100k
Reports to	Chief Technical Officer
Education	Bachelor of IT from [some local college].
Count of staff	Team of 5 people.
PERFORMANCE MEASURES (2)	
Performance measures	# satisfied clients, # resolved support requests, # improved processes, workplace morale.
BIO (3)	
Bio	Lou worked in a cafe while doing an IT degree at [some local college], is a gamer, and takes pride in customer service.
QUOTE (4)	
Quote	I like being part of the solution, not the problem.
MOTIVATIONS (5)	
Values: What is important to them? What drives the decisions they make?	**Teamwork:** Build a happy and cohesive team. **Ideology:** Customer satisfaction and being the helpful face of the business.
ROLE AND RESPONSIBILITY (6)	
Overseeing support staff (50%)	Monitor that support requests are being dealt with professionally and timely.

HEADING	Your hiring manager – suggestions for answers
Improving documentation (30%)	Improving system and user documentation based on reports from support staff.

Meetings (20%)	Meetings to discuss...
	    Problem support tickets.
	    Support area performance.
	    Support area structure.

GOALS (7)	
Customer experience	Improve the customer experience by improving documentation. Improved feedback to developers to make Moodle-4-K-12 more user friendly.
Staff training	Improve support tickets resolution time. Rotate development and support areas to improve the quality of support.
FRUSTRATIONS (8)	
Staff training.	Too much time spent on escalated support issues that front line staff should be capable of dealing with.
Ticketing	Staff not using ticketing system correctly. Makes performance analysis of support area inaccurate.
Constraints	Understaffed. Narrow skillset of staff
INFLUENCES (9)	
Influences	Competitors, edwiser blog, Moodle blog, Martin Dougiamas (Moodle founder).
SOFTWARE (10)	
Office suite, CRM, ...	Microsoft Office Moodle Zendesk Monday PHP, JavaScript, HTML5, SQL and HTTP

Avatar for the workplace Alex's IT job is within

Table 12: IT workplace avatar: See numbers in Figure 8.

HEADING	The business – suggestions for answers
OVERVIEW (1)	
Photo: Find a photo that represents a widget they sell, service they provide, or logo.	MOODLE -4-K-12 Insert logo.
Name: Business name	Moodle-4-K-12
Time in business.	5 years.
Employees.	10 office staff, 10 developers, 1 sales engineer, 2 implementation engineers, 5 support staff.
Income.	$6m annual revenue.
PERFORMANCE MEASURES (2)	
Performance measures	Annual growth >15%. Raving customers.
BIO (3)	
Bio.	Moodle-4-K-12 is a market leading provider of Moodle LMS solutions for mid size K-12 schools. Our clients are just big enough to need an LMS, but too small to employ their own LMS workforce. We distribute and support our own Moodle solution. We support teachers so they can get on with teaching and their students can get on with learning.
QUOTE (4)	
Quote.	Education tech without the tech talk.
MOTIVATIONS (5)	
Growth.	Growth via new clients and new offerings.
Values: What is important to them? What drives the decisions they make?	**Ideology:** Ensure adherence to company standards. **Teamwork:** Build a happy and cohesive team. **Quality:** Aim to build a body of raving fans.

HEADING	The business – suggestions for answers
Clients (6)	
Clients.	Typical clients are 300-1000 student schools.
Client pain points and frustrations. What brings them to the business?	Technology overload. Setting up the system. Insufficient technical knowledge.
Geography.	Eastern metro.
GOALS (7)	
Systems.	Online help videos. Better systems to capture client feedback.
Support.	Introduce gold, silver and bronze support packages.
Staff	Rotate staff to overcome compartmentalized knowledge.
FRUSTRATIONS (8)	
Hard to find qualified staff.	Recruiting staff is time consuming and extra work.
Office.	Need better coordination between teams.
Current processes complicated and stressful.	Too much time spent on managing projects.
Feedback.	Feedback from clients not making its way to developers.
Lack of expertise.	We're rolling out system upgrades, but clients are not using them.
Constraints.	Not enough staff understand the entire system.
EMPLOYEE BENEFITS (9)	
Benefits.	20 days annual leave, Public holidays, 10 days sick leave, Pension fund, Flexible hours, Work at home or office.
SOFTWARE (10)	
Office suite, CRM, ...	Microsoft Office. Xero accounting. Monday project management. Moodle LMS. Zendesk support ticketing. PHP, JavaScript, HTML5, SQL and HTTP

Figure 7: The IT hiring manager avatar graphic. See numbers in Table 11.

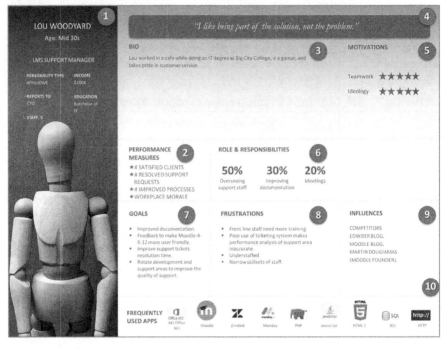

Figure 8: The IT business avatar graphic. See numbers in Table 12.

Alex's LinkedIn Profile: It has a Moodle focus

The information below is discussed in detail in the LinkedIn section. The capitalized letters relate to those in Figure 4.

Contact information (A)

- **Profile Name:** alex-johnson-lms
- **Email:** alex-johnson-lms@somedomain.com
- **Website:** ripn.org/lms

Job preferences (B)

- Check the box to say that you're looking for work.

Intro section (C)

- **Basic information:** Fill in obvious things like name, location, industry, education.
- **Headline:** IT graduate seeking entry level LMS position
- **Photo:** Friendly and consistent with other Moodle-4-K-12 staff you find on LinkedIn.

About (D)

Hi. I'm Alex

I'm fascinated by LMSs. I used Moodle as both a student and as a teacher when I helped my college professor teach the Introduction to LMS class for IT 101. I am also the Moodle coordinator and administrator at the Regional Indigenous Plant Nursery (RIPN), a not for profit that, as well as other things, runs courses about indigenous vegetation.

I wireframed and then created the lesson structure for the two instructors to add their resources into. I also wrote an import plugin in PHP that retained one instructor's lesson formatting. 8 students enrolled in the first course and 6 in the other.

Instructors and students liked the help videos I made using Camtasia. I also created help documents in word using Snagit for screen captures and text files extracted from the videos using ai.

Recently the site was awarded the annual Community Education Prize by the National Indigenous Vegetation Society.

Featured content (E)

- Interesting blog posts that Alex read about LMS in the not-for-profit sector.
- Links to LMS examples and sites that resonate: Moodle.org AND elearningindustry.com/use-moodle-business-10-ways
- Youtube presentations with voiceover commentary.
- Selected tutorial videos for RIPN students.
- College presentations about the impact of LMS on community groups.

Work experience (G)

Regional Indigenous Plant Nursery. [March 2020] – present (part time). Moodle LMS coordinator and administrator...

- System setup.
- Site wireframing and lesson template setup.
- Exam setup.
- Teacher and student account, and email setup.
- Wrote an import plugin in PHP.
- Help videos
- Help documentation seeded by transcriptions extracted from videos using ai.

Education (H)

Bachelor's degree in IT at [some local college]. I used the Regional Indigenous Plant Nursery Moodle site I built for my class project. My favorite part of the course was building a PHP plugin to import an instructor's lessons into Moodle so that the word documents retained their formatting.

Skills, endorsements and recommendations (I)

Add skills such as Moodle and IT support.

Alex presented Regional Indigenous Plant Nursery as an LMS example at the *National Indigenous Vegetation Conference* (see accomplishments section), and asked attendees for endorsements and recommendations. Alex also asked a college lecturer, members of Regional Indigenous Plant Nursery, and course teachers for endorsements.

Accomplishments (K)

Feature presenter on LMS at the 2021 National Indigenous Vegetation Conference.

Interests (L)

Alex follows LMS influencers like Moodle LMS founder (Martin Dougiamas) and the Moodle company.

Alex is a member of the Moodle, and *System Admin* groups.

Alex's Cover letter: Moodle Level 1 Support

Position number: 1234
Date: MM/DD/YYYY
Alex Johnson
E: alex.johnson@somedomain.com
T: 0123456789
L: linkedin.com/in/alex-johnson-lms
A: Suburb

Lou Woodyard
Moodle-4-K-12
Moodle-4-K-12 address

Dear Lou

Thank you for your invitation to apply for the graduate marketing position at Moodle-4-K-12. I am a recent graduate in IT from [college name].

I'm fascinated by LMSs. I have experienced Moodle as a student and as a teacher when I helped my college professor teach the Introduction to LMS class for IT 101. I am also the Moodle coordinator and administrator at the Regional Indigenous Plant Nursery (RIPN), a not for profit that, among other things, runs courses about indigenous vegetation.

At RIPN I wireframed and then created the lesson structure for the two instructors to add their resources into. I also wrote an import plugin in PHP that retained one instructor's word document lesson formatting. 8 students enrolled in the first course and 6 in the other. I setup the site and then I administered it.

I enjoy customer service work. Instructors and students liked the help videos I made using Camtasia. I created help documents in word using Snagit for screen captures. These were seeded by transcripts extracted from the videos using ai. It was satisfying to see the drastic drop in support requests that occurred after I launched the LMS help system.

In 2021 the site was awarded the annual Community Education Prize by the National Indigenous Vegetation Society.

Building the RIPN site and seeing it become a genuine success story is the most satisfying thing I've ever done. Being part of a team that was awarded a national prize was gratifying. Recently I began training an intern from my college to maintain the LMS when I move on.

I sense that many of the things I have learned through my involvement with RIPN are directly relevant to Moodle-4-K-12's needs. My RIPN experience has given me a taste of the education sector. The opportunity for a career working with K-12 schools is an exciting prospect for me. I feel like I have the self-taught Moodle basics to build on and I would dearly love to learn how a Moodle shop goes about setting up and maintaining an LMS site. I have also completed Moodle and Zendesk MOOCs, and so it is my belief that I would be useful in a support role from day 1.

Thank you for your time and consideration. I look forward to meeting with you to discuss your exciting position in person.

Yours Sincerely,

Alex Johnson

E:	Alex.Johnson@somedomain.com
T:	0123456789
L:	linkedin.com/in/alex-johnson-lms
W:	ripn.org/lms
Encl:	Alex-Johnson-Graduate-LMS-Resume.docx
	Alex-Johnson-Graduate-LMS-Resume.pdf

Alex's résumé: Moodle Specialist

Alex Johnson,
Moodle Specialist

E: alex.johnson@somedomain.com
T: 0123456789
L: linkedin.com/in/alex-johnson-lms
[Suburb]

EXECUTIVE SUMMARY

I am a Moodle specialist. I am a recent graduate and I already have one success. I have been coordinator and administrator for *Regional Indigenous Plant Nursery's (RIPN)* Moodle Learning Management System (LMS) since March 2019. During that time, I coordinated the launch of two courses. Recently the site received a national education award. I was able to work professionally and constructively with the RIPN board and two instructors to create the courses. It was a challenging project for an organization that had not delivered courses online before. I also setup exams, produced help videos and documentation and trained the instructors to make the video lessons using Camtasia and Snagit. I learned a lot about being patient in support situations. The final year of my degree was delivered remotely, demonstrating that I am able to work independently. Recently I completed Moodle and Zendesk MOOCs.

EXPERTISE

- **Wireframing**
- **PHP**
- **Project Planning**
- **Moodle support**
- **Help documentation**
- **Help videos**

WORK HISTORY

Regional Indigenous Plant Nursery March 2020–September 2021 (part time)

RIPN is a not for profit run by a committee of 6. It is the indigenous vegetation peak body for the state's south east (26,000 sq miles). There is one full time staff member, 40 volunteers, and 2 instructors. During my time there I completed the design, build and implementation of a Moodle LMS for two courses. I then supported and produced help videos and other documentation. The first intake was 14 students.

Moodle coordinator, Administrator and IT support engineer

Successfully managed the full range of relationships (RIPN board, Instructors and students) to launch two courses using the Moodle LMS.

- **System setup:** Worked with instructors to wireframe, coordinate user testing and implement ripn.org/lms.
- **App writing:** Wrote a PHP app to import an instructor's coursework in a way that maintained its formatting.
- **IT Support:** I was help desk for the moodle installation. I provided troubleshooting and IT support to instructors and students via email and moodle chat. IT support included account creation, email setup, etc.
- **Help videos:** Created help videos using Camtasia. System related support queries reduced significantly.
- **Help documentation:** Extracted audio files from help videos and sent then for ai transcription. I used the transcripts and Snagit screen captures to create help documentation.

[college name]   August 2020 (part time)

Assisted with the delivery of the *introduction to LMS* section of IT 101. Orientation for first year students to using the college LMS as a student, as well as general Moodle features.

Sam's Fuel Station   November 2015–September 2021 (part time)

Sam's Fuel Station is a 14 bay fuel depot. Three staff are always on duty.

Console operator

I worked as a console operator and general help.

- Computer system support.
- Inventory management and supply ordering
- Till balance
- Console operation

EDUCATION AND QUALIFICATIONS

Bachelor of IT [college name]   August 2018–June 2021

The course covered a range of IT topics, including languages like PHP, JavaScript, HTML5, SQL and HTTP, as well as basic server maintenance.

ADDITIONAL TRAINING

- **Moodle MOOCs:** Moodle admin basics, Moodle plugin development basics.
- **Zendesk MOOCs:** Zendesk support for agents 1, Zendesk overview for agents.
- **Youtube:** Addition Zendesk and Moodle training videos.
- Software:
    - **Beginner:** Zendesk
    - **Intermediate:** PHP, JavaScript, HTML5, Camtasia, Snagit.
    - **Advanced:** Word, Excel, PowerPoint, Moodle.

ADDITIONAL SKILLS

- Feature presenter on LMS at the 2021 National Indigenous Vegetation Conference

REFERENCES

My referees have requested that I provide their details only if requested in the final stages of recruitment.

Job application example 3: PARALLEL UNIVERSE #6 – Accounting graduate

Accounting is a high stakes career. Errors (accidental or deliberate) can make a business appear to be performing better or worse than it actually is. So, additional qualifications, registrations, and even licenses are required for accountants to act in some roles. Hence, graduates tend to start at the bottom and work under close supervision on simple tasks when they start out. The thing is, all those simple tasks, someone has to do them!

Alex's work experience this time is as a bookkeeper in a small builder's hardware business. It's just big enough to employ a full time accountant who's overworked and so grateful for any help they can get. In such an environment, Alex gets exposed to a wide range of business roles.

Bookkeeping jobs like that are easy to come by, even by knocking on business' doors. Becoming a tax volunteer would have been another option. They help the underprivileged with their tax returns. Most countries do this, and the position usually comes with training and supervision. Google *tax volunteer [your country]* to find out more.

THE AD – WANTED: Accounting graduate

Truckin Stuff has been a national truck parts manufacturer and distributor since 2005. We have a strong order book and have recently grown through an opportunistic acquisition of Truckin Bits. We now have over 250 staff in 30 locations across the country. It's an exciting time to be working at Truckin Stuff. The acquisition has created many challenges, the biggest of which is the integration of Truckin Bit's business systems into ours. We are using the acquisition as an opportunity to move the business into an, as yet undecided, Enterprise Resource Planning (ERP) system.

The position

Our recent growth has created an opportunity for a graduate accountant. This is an entry-level position. We acknowledge that at this stage of your career your experience may be limited.

You will report to the company accountant who works closely with our management team to assist in the daily running and the continued growth of the business. Close to the action, you will be mentored into opportunities that align with your strengths so you can develop into the professional you seek to be!

You will assist with (but not limited to) the following...

- Internal reporting, including processing bank transactions into the accounting system.
- Ensure overhead expenses are correctly allocated including wages, phones, tolls, fuel.
- Support business units to minimize aged debtors.
- Preparation and processing of adjusting journals.
- Monthly general ledger account reconciliations.
- General ledger maintenance and trial balance.
- Fixed asset register maintenance.
- Statutory reporting.
- Payroll.

Key competencies

The ideal candidate will have...

- Accounting/Commerce or equivalent degree (or near completion).
- Proven ability to problem solve effectively.
- Strong written and verbal communication skills.
- Strong ability and confidence to engage with stakeholders.
- Strong MS Office skills.
- Excellent attention to detail.
- Familiarity with Enterprise Resource Planning systems.
- Previous experience in a business context would be advantageous – this may have been achieved through vacation work in a relevant industry and/or part time work while studying.

Benefits

- A respected growing organization.
- Support and guidance from senior staff.
- A positive and rewarding team culture.
- Future career progression where great work is recognized and rewarded.
- Up to date technology.
- Comfortable and modern office setting.
- Flexible working arrangements.
- Convenient on-site parking.
- Attractive salary offering.

If you are a highly motivated individual looking to kick off your career then we would love to hear from you! Please forward your cover letter and résumé to lou-woodyard@truckinstuff.com.

Avatar for Alex's Accounting hiring manager

Table 13: Accounting hiring manager avatar. See numbers in Figure 9

HEADING	Truckin Stuff Accountant – suggestions for answers
OVERVIEW (1)	
Photo of someone who looks like your boss (or a photo of the actual person).	Photo of Lou. Or a stock photo (e.g. pxhere.com, freeimages.com, commons.wikimedia.org). Only use famous people if that's who you're aspiring to work for.
Name	Lou Woodyard.
Age	Late 40s.
Job title	Company accountant.
Personality traits	Affiliate [personality trait from Table 5].
Income	$180k.
Reports to	CEO.
Education	Bachelor of Accounting from [some local college]. CPA.
Count of staff	Team of 3 people (staff accountant, admin/book keeper, graduate accountant).
PERFORMANCE MEASURES (2)	
Performance measures	Timely reports, accurate reports, zero tax problems, improved processes, successful Truckin Bits integration.
BIO (3)	
Bio	While studying Lou worked in a cafe and then as a book keeper in a small business.
QUOTE (4)	
Quote	Behind every good business is a great accountant.
MOTIVATIONS (5)	
Values: What is important to them? What drives the decisions they make?	**Business health:** Robust business systems. Timely financial reporting. **Business growth:** Removing obstacles to growth.

HEADING	Truckin Stuff Accountant – suggestions for answers
ROLE AND RESPONSIBILITY (6)	
Overseeing junior staff (30%)	Supervise and support junior staff.
Improving systems (40%)	• Improve system and user documentation. • Review and document all systems in Truckin Bits and Truckin Stuff. • Create ERP system specification. • Review ERP functionality for fit and propose a short list of candidates. • Purchase ERP. • Rollout ERP.
Asset register (10%)	Review for the Truckin Stuff and Truckin Bits businesses.
Meetings (20%)	• Meetings to discuss... • Acquisition. • Business finances. • ERP. • Upcoming board meetings. • Statutory reporting.
GOALS (7)	
Smooth acquisition	Ensure the Truckin Bits acquisition does not impact on... • Staff satisfaction. • Customer satisfaction.
Staff training	Smooth implementation of ERP. Train staff to use ERP. Train staff to use new business systems.
FRUSTRATIONS (8)	
Outdated systems and software	Too much time spent on moving figures between computer systems that don't talk to each other.
Incompatible systems	Different accounting systems in Truckin Bits and Truckin Stuff. Integration is going to be tricky.
Constraints	Understaffed. Narrow skillset of staff.
INFLUENCES (9)	
Influences	Competitors, Ray Dalio (business author), Naomi Simson (entrepreneur)
SOFTWARE (10)	
Office suite, accounting system, project management...	Microsoft Office, Quicken, ERP (undecided)., Monday.

Avatar for the workplace Alex's Accounting job is within

Table 14: Accounting workplace avatar. See numbers in Figure 10.

HEADING	The Truckin Stuff business – suggestions for answers
OVERVIEW (1)	
Photo: Find a photo that represents a widget they sell, service they provide, or logo.	TRUCKIN STUFF
Name: Business name	Truckin Stuff.
Time in business.	16 years.
Employees.	250 (30 office staff, 120 manufacturing, 100 warehousing & distribution).
Income.	$68m annual revenue.
PERFORMANCE MEASURES (2)	
Performance measures	Annual growth >15%. Staff working as a team. Raving customers.
BIO (3)	
Bio.	Truckin Stuff is a family business that has grown. We're meeting a need for locally made truck parts.
QUOTE (4)	
Quote.	Locally made and on the move.
MOTIVATIONS (5)	
Growth.	Growth via new clients, new offerings, and acquisitions.
Values: What is important to them? What drives the decisions they make?	**Ideology:** Ensure adherence to company standards. **Teamwork:** Build a happy and cohesive team. **Quality:** Aim to build a body of raving fans. Parts that exceed national standards.
Clients (6)	
Clients.	Typically mid size transport companies.

HEADING	The Truckin Stuff business – suggestions for answers
Client pain points and frustrations. What brings them to the business?	Long wait times for Genuine spare parts. Expense of Genuine spare parts. Big brands not interested in selling parts for older trucks.
Geography.	National.
GOALS (7)	
Systems.	Better systems to capture client feedback. Customer relationship management systems. Better online purchasing options. Better corporate information systems.
Support.	Better post-sales support.
Staff.	Integrate staff from Truckin Bits and Truckin Stuff.
Growth.	Acquire suppliers to improve reliability of supply.
FRUSTRATIONS (8)	
Compliance.	Manufacturing and office ISO standards, labor, tax.
Suppliers.	Some are unreliable.
Debt collection.	Collecting from non payers.
Minutiae.	Too much time dealing with spot fires and too little time being strategic. Too many staff wearing too many hats.
Equipment.	Too much old equipment that's unreliable or incompatible, and affecting productivity.
Constraints.	Not enough staff understand the entire system.
EMPLOYEE BENEFITS (9)	
Benefits.	**Everyone:** 20 days annual leave, Public holidays, 10 days sick leave, Pension fund. **For office staff add:** Flexible hours, Work at home or office.
SOFTWARE (10)	
Office suite, CRM, ...	Microsoft Office. Quicken. Monday project management. Unknown ERP.

Figure 9: The Accounting hiring manager avatar graphic. See numbers in Table 13

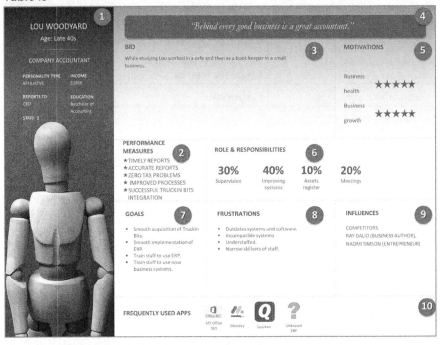

Figure 10: The Accounting workplace avatar graphic. See numbers in Table 14.

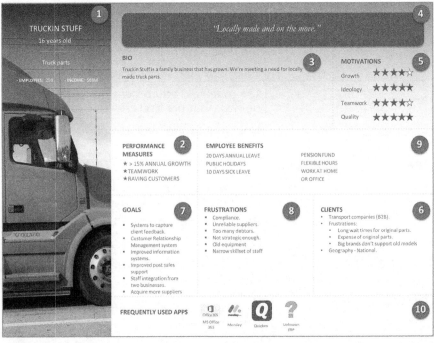

Alex's LinkedIn Profile: It has a focus on accounting and ERPs

The information below is discussed in detail in the LinkedIn section. The capitalized letters relate to those in Figure 4.

Contact information (A)

- Profile Name: alex-johnson-accountant
- Email: alex-johnson@somedomain.com

Job preferences (B)

Check the box to say that you're looking for work.

Intro section (C)

Basic information: Fill in obvious things like name, location, industry, education.

Headline: Accounting graduate seeking entry level accounting position

Photo: Friendly and consistent with other Truckin Stuff staff you find on LinkedIn.

About (D)

Hi. I'm Alex

Even in primary school I was excited by numbers. In high school I was always the best in my class at maths. My love of numbers led me to study accounting.

In my final year at college I worked as a bookkeeper in Nuts n Bolts, a small builder's hardware company. As assistant to a busy accountant I got to do a greater range of work than many of my class mates who were doing formal internships in large accounting firms.

Nuts n Bolts was hampered by outdated systems and excel spreadsheet silos. I was tasked with doing a preliminary investigation for cloud based ERP candidates. Armed with a brief to "avoid software that would be a sledgehammer to crack a nut", the challenge was to find a modular solution that was appropriate

---

for the business in terms of cost, functionality, and Nuts n Bolts ability to roll it out using its own resources.

After a detailed review, the company accountant chose the Odoo ERP from my shortlist. Its impact on Nuts n Bolts was eye opening. It freed data from Excel silos and centralized it. There was no more double handling of data and so human errors were near-eliminated. The system quickly paid its way because one admin worker was freed to do more strategic work.

Featured content (E)

- Interesting blog posts that Alex read about cloud solutions for Enterprise Resource Planning systems.
- Voiceover PowerPoint of ERP college presentation.

Work experience (G)

Nuts n bolts. [March 2020] – present (part time). Book keeper (part time)...

- Maintenance of fixed assets register.
- Assistance with payroll.
- Documentation of processes.
- Monthly report of aged debtors.
- Strategic review of ERP requirements

Education (H)

Bachelor's degree in accounting at [some local college]. My favorite part of the course was my elective project about ERPs. I never imagined myself being excited about technology. I used my bookkeeping job at Nuts n Bolts as case study.

Skills, endorsements and recommendations (I)

Add skills such as Odoo, Quicken and MS Office.

Alex presented the Nuts n Bolts ERP research to the local Chamber of Commerce breakfast meeting (see accomplishments section), and asked attendees for endorsements and recommendations. Alex also asked a lecturer from college, the Nuts n Bolts accountant, plus course teachers for endorsements.

Accomplishments (K)

Business breakfast presenter at the local Chamber of Commerce September 2021 breakfast meeting. Topic was Enterprise Resource Planning systems and small business.

Interests (L)

Alex is a member of the ERP Community, ERP professionals, Accounting finance professionals and Accounting and audit groups.

Alex's Cover letter: Accounting graduate

Position number: 1234
Date: MM/DD/YYYY
Alex Johnson
E: alex.johnson@somedomain.com
T: 0123456789
L: linkedin.com/in/alex-johnson-
  accountant
A: Suburb

Lou Woodyard
Truckin Stuff
Truckin Stuff address

Dear Lou

Thank you for your invitation to apply for the graduate accounting position at Truckin Stuff. I am a recent graduate in accounting from [college name].

I am one of those people who loves numbers. That's what led me to study accounting.

While at college I worked as a bookkeeper in a small builder's hardware business called Nuts n Bolts. As assistant to a busy accountant I got to do a wide range of work.

I worked throughout the Nuts n Bolts business. I assisted with journaling, maintaining the fixed assets register, payroll, bank reconciliation, and identifying aged debtors. I enjoyed the variety of tasks and people. As a communicator, I was good at getting store staff to work with me to resolve issues I was sent to deal with. I gained experience with till balancing and till technology.

Nuts n Bolts was hampered by outdated systems and excel spreadsheet silos. I was tasked with doing a preliminary investigation for cloud based ERP candidates. Armed with a brief to "avoid software that would be a sledgehammer to crack a nut", the challenge was to find a modular solution that was appropriate for the business in terms of cost, functionality, and Nuts n Bolts' ability to roll it out using its own resources.

After a detailed review, the company accountant chose my preferred ERP, Odoo. Its impact on Nuts n Bolts was eye opening. It freed data from Excel silos and centralized it. There was no more double handling of data and so human errors were near-eliminated. Consequently, the business ran more efficiently and the company accountant was less overworked. The system quickly paid its way because one admin worker was freed to do more strategic work.

I used my Nuts n Bolts ERP experience as a case study for my final year major project and was awarded an A grade for it.

My Nuts n Bolts experience has been fun and rewarding. I feel I am ready for a new challenge. I would love to learn how a bigger shop goes about choosing, setting up and rolling out an ERP system. I have completed Odoo's online training and worked on Nuts n Bolts ERP implementation. I believe my understanding of ERPs, and the breadth of my experience at Nuts n Bolts will make me useful to Truckin Stuff from day 1.

Thank you for your time and consideration. I look forward to meeting with you to discuss your exciting position in person.

Yours Sincerely,

Alex Johnson

E:	Alex.Johnson@somedomain.com
T:	0123456789
L:	linkedin.com/in/alex-johnson-accountant
Encl:	Alex-Johnson-Graduate-Accountant-Resume.docx
	Alex-Johnson-Graduate-Accountant-Resume.pdf

Alex's résumé: Accounting graduate

**Alex Johnson,
Accountant**

E: alex.johnson@somedomain.com
T: 0123456789
L: linkedin.com/in/alex-johnson-
accountant
[Suburb]

EXECUTIVE SUMMARY

I am an accounting graduate and worked my way through college as a bookkeeper in a small builders hardware supplier called Nuts n Bolts. During my time there I worked closely with the company accountant and assisted with fixed assets register, payroll, identifying aged debtors, documentation of processes, and ERP review and rollout. I also documented the payroll system as a part of the ERP rollout. I'm good with spreadsheets and can code formulas. I am also familiar with Quicken. My special interest is ERPs and I recently delivered a breakfast meeting presentation on ERPs for small business. The ERP rollout at Nuts n Bolts freed up one staff member to work on more strategic projects, and improved the reliability and timeliness of business reporting. The final year of my degree was delivered remotely, demonstrating that I am able to work unsupervised. Recently I completed over 30 hours of Odoo online training.

EXPERTISE

- **Maintenance of fixed assets register.**
- **Payroll.**
- **Documentation of processes.**
- **Aged debtors reporting.**
- **ERP**

WORK HISTORY

Nuts n Bolts   March 2019–Present (part time)

Nuts n Bolts *is a small builders hardware business with 6 office staff and 10 warehouse/shop staff. There's lots of inventory, lots of transactions and big customer service requirements. I assist with all aspects of the accountant's daily work.*

Bookkeeper

I work closely with the company accountant on day to day and strategic problems.

- **Fixed assets register maintenance:** Enter details of business assets and monitor their depreciation status.
- **Payroll:** Maintain payroll system so that employees are paid correctly and labor and tax obligations are fulfilled.
- **Documentation of processes:** Documented the payroll system so it could be duplicated in the ERP.
- **Aged debtors reporting:** Produced end-of-week aged debtor reports for review by the accountant.
- **Strategic ERP review:** Produced a strategic review of cloud based ERP systems in preparation for a more detailed investigation by the company accountant.

EDUCATION AND QUALIFICATIONS

Bachelor of Accounting [college name]   August 2018–June 2021

The course covered a range of accounting topics, including Journaling, Technology (cloud accounting systems, ERP, Excel), profit and loss, assets register and trial balance. My major project was about ERPs.

SKILLS

- **Odoo training:** Odoo online courses (~30 hours).
- Software:
  - **Intermediate:** Quicken, Odoo.
  - **Advanced:** Word, Excel, PowerPoint.

REFERENCES

My referees have requested that I provide their details only if requested in the final stages of recruitment.

Appendix
List of web pages on the companion website

Description	Length mm:ss	bit.ly link
Preface	8:49	https://bit.ly/wsjsd-0-1
Introduction	17:06	https://bit.ly/wsjsd-0-2
Part 1 – Overview	28:16	https://bit.ly/wsjsd-1-1
Part 2.1 – Introduction to Part Two	3:17	https://bit.ly/wsjsd-2-1
Part 2.2 – How to do Industry Research	10:10	https://bit.ly/wsjsd-2-2
Part 2.3 –How to create an Avatar of your Hiring Manager and Workplace	13:43	https://bit.ly/wsjsd-2-3
Part 2.4 – LinkedIn Introduction	9:04	https://bit.ly/wsjsd-2-4
Part 2.5 – LinkedIn nuts-n-bolts	42:11	https://bit.ly/wsjsd-2-5
Part 2.6 – Wrapping up your Presence Pyramid Levels 1 and 2	4:57	https://bit.ly/wsjsd-2-6
Part 2.7 – How to network and build relationships	50:11	https://bit.ly/wsjsd-2-7
Part 3.1 – Introduction to Part Three	6:28	https://bit.ly/wsjsd-3-1
Part 3.2 – How to apply for a Job	41:18	https://bit.ly/wsjsd-3-2
Part 4.1 – Worked example of converting a Marketing Manager Avatar table to a graphic	7:18	https://bit.ly/wsjsd-4-1
Total	**4:08**	

Goodreads review page		https://bit.ly/Job-Hunting-Book-Goodreads

NOTES:

NOTES:

NOTES:

Printed in Great Britain
by Amazon

27112238R00110